Praise for
NO EXPLANATION REQUIRED!

"No Explanation Required! encourages women to be unapologetically ambitious. Using personal insights and research-backed strategies, Carol Sankar offers effective tools for pushing back on the biases that block progress for women at work. This is a much-needed message on how you can find your voice and thrive in the workplace."

—Sheryl Sandberg, COO of Facebook and founder of Lean In

"In her book, *No Explanation Required!*, Carol Sankar creates a space for ambitious women to really acknowledge and overcome the kind of limiting beliefs and internalized sexism that hinders the career advancement of many women today. Filled with relatable stories and practical solutions, this book helps us learn how to navigate the dualities of what it means to be a woman and a leader in the workplace. By including concepts like the K.I.S.S. Principle and the 8-Minute Rule, along with scripts and confidence building activities, Carol equips women everywhere with the tools, terms, and techniques needed to be seen heard and respected anywhere. This book was truly an eye-opening, personally empowering read."

—LaShanda Henry, online business coach and founder of SistaSense for Women Entrepreneurs

"No Explanation Required! is a book that ambitious women need NOW. Carol brilliantly wrote this book filled with data and relevant stories of why women aren't standing in their full power to ask for what they deserve. The challenges that women experience in the workplace start long before we even graduate high school and the flurry of double standards during our careers make it difficult for

women to ascend up the ladder of success. This book will clear the path for women to excel in their careers and shatter the glass ceiling that has plagued ambitious women for long enough. Bravo Carol for offering the masterpiece to the world!"

—Christy Rutherford, advisor to executive leaders and founder of ChristyRutherford.com

"This book completely blew my mind and surpassed my high expectations. *No Explanation Required!* is like having a conversation with your best friend, mentor, and biggest truth teller all at once. You know Carol Sankar has your back because she is sharing her own struggles, then she gives you a road map to help you get out of your own way. If you are motivated to get to higher grounds and do the work, this is the road map and tangible advice you have been looking for. You are worth fighting for, and it starts with you."

—Edwige A. Robinson, expert technologist and transformational senior leader

NO EXPLANATION REQUIRED!

NO EXPLANATION REQUIRED!

A WOMAN'S GUIDE TO ASSERT
YOUR CONFIDENCE AND
COMMUNICATE TO WIN AT WORK

CAROL SANKAR

New York Chicago San Francisco Athens London Madrid
Mexico City Milan New Delhi Singapore Sydney Toronto

1 2 3 4 5 6 7 8 9   LCR   26 25 24 23 22 21

ISBN   978-1-260-47484-8
MHID   1-260-47484-4

e-ISBN 978-1-260-47485-5
e-MHID   1-260-47485-2

Library of Congress Cataloging-in-Publication Data

Names: Sankar, Carol, author.
Title: No explanation required : a woman's guide to assert your confidence and
    communicate to win at work / Carol Sankar.
Description: New York : McGraw Hill, [2022] | Includes bibliographical references
    and index.
Identifiers: LCCN 2021037357 (print) | LCCN 2021037358 (ebook) | ISBN
    9781260474848 (hardcover) | ISBN 9781260474855 (ebook)
Subjects: LCSH: Business communication. | Women—Communication. |
    Self-esteem in women. | Confidence.
Classification: LCC HF5718 .S255 2021 (print) | LCC HF5718 (ebook) |
    DDC 651.7—dc23
LC record available at https://lccn.loc.gov/2021037357
LC ebook record available at https://lccn.loc.gov/2021037358

McGraw Hill books are available at special quantity discounts to use as premiums and sales promotions or for use in corporate training programs. To contact a representative, please visit the Contact Us pages at www.mhprofessional.com.

To Yvonne Joseph-Callender

Thank you for your limitless love.

*Thank you for prioritizing my dreams, even
if you didn't understand them.*

I miss you so much!

I live to make you proud every day.

To Mr. Sankar

Thank you for your patience.

*Thank you for listening, although you
didn't always understand.*

Thank you for the espresso shots (laughing).

*Thank you for taking some of the responsibilities
off of my plate, so I could win!*

Thank you for your love!

CONTENTS

Acknowledgments   ix

Introduction: The Language of Hope   1

1 **The Self-Promotion Gap!**   17
Creating a Winning Perception

2 **Perception and Performance**   37
Creating a Cycle of Professionalism

3 **What's Like Got to Do with It?**   55
The Rewards of Respect

4 **Activating Your Alter Ego**   75
A Super Power for Performance

5 **Women-Centered Stereotypes**   91
How to Break Out of the "Norm"

6 **Communicating in a Crisis**   113
The Difference Between Reaction and Response

7 **Sorry for What?**   137
Avoiding the Passive Apology

8 **The Power and Precision of Prepositions**   159
Learning the Little Words That Go a Long Way

9 **The 8-Minute Rule**   167
Mastering the Art of Micro Conversations

It's A Wrap!   191

References   207

Index   213

ACKNOWLEDGMENTS

There is not enough room to thank all of the people who have been a sounding board in my life and patient with me through this process. I wrote this book in the midst of so many life challenges, but I'm so glad I was surrounded with nothing but love to get through it and see my dream come to fruition.

I am eternally grateful for the two most important men in my life: Thanks to my husband for believing in my dreams and clapping louder for me than I do for myself. He has allowed me the space and time to be creative and focus, while remaining compassionate with my mood swings. Thank you to my son, who has been right there every step of the way, while making me laugh to take a break from writing. I'm thankful for all of the mommy and son time we've had during this process, while in quarantine. He's truly the best son a mother could have. I love you both so much.

To my family: aunts, uncles, and cousins who have been praying for me during this process. Your guidance has been a source of strength and comfort. Thank you for sharing my work and sending me all of your well wishes.

I wish my grandparents were still here to share this moment. I feel their love and blessings over my life daily. I've worn my grandparents' wedding bands on my necklace, and held them close to my heart for guidance and protection.

Without their sacrifice, my success wouldn't have been possible.

To my dearest cousin, T.J.: Thank you for being my big sister. All of our lives, it has always felt like it was just us. Thank you for sharing stories about Granny that helped me write this book. More importantly, your support means the world.

I'm grateful for all of the mentors who have played a role or planted a seed in my life—Selma Jackson, Samantha Brown, Ms. Ellis, Dr. Meena Bose, Dr. Juanita Richardson, Dr. Bridget Welch, Jamie Kern Lima, Ryan Serhant, Rohini Dey, Debra Wabnik-Hope, Barbara Corcoran, my editorial families at *Inc.* magazine and *Entrepreneur* magazine, and many more that have personally impacted and invested in my success over the years.

To my friends, advisors, and colleagues: Thanks for making me laugh. There were many days I wanted to throw my laptop through the window and hide. You kept assuring me that there are people who need to know the importance of No Explanation Required!

To Starbucks, Trader Joe's, and Maxwell House: Thank you for keeping me awake at night so I could keep writing, thinking, and editing. Caffeine played a major role in my creativity, and without you, late-night writing sessions would not have been possible. You've all kept me going, especially with a double shot of espresso and matcha tea—it's a must.

I am also thankful for some of the traumatic and toxic workplace behaviors that helped me find my voice and learn the importance of self-advocacy.

I am grateful for everyone who rejected me, laughed, and told me to be realistic. I am negatively motivated, and I used it as fuel to succeed. In the words of Beyoncé, "You're the best thing I never had." Thank you for doubting me, while peeking at my timeline and stories on social media. I don't take anything personally, but I am grateful that I don't allow rejection to stop me.

I am grateful for my amazing editors and team at McGraw Hill. You are absolutely the best!

Lastly, I am overwhelmed by the support of my team at The Confidence Factor for Women. The gifts and words of encouragement kept me going when sleepiness started kicking in. Thank you for giving me the time and space I needed, while taking so many tasks off of my plate, especially when I was close to the finish line.

INTRODUCTION

The Language of Hope

I've come a long way from the Brooklyn girl donning a double ponytail, sitting on the front steps, in a Catholic school uniform, on Foster Avenue. The first generation in my family to be raised in the United States, I was nicknamed "The Hope." My grandparents emigrated to the United States in the late 1970s from Trinidad and Tobago with the hope that they could create equitable opportunities for their daughters and granddaughters. With her roots ingrained in conservative gender roles, my grandmother struggled to embrace the idea that women could lead or have equal access to executive-level opportunities. By the time I was in grade school, television and movies portrayed strong women, albeit with a man or two behind them, managing them ... just in case. A triad of "angels," a "bionic" woman, even a "female" detective (can you believe women could be cops?), half-convincingly showed women could be strong and lead, but always with a chaperone, a man behind the scenes (sometimes only a voice) to manage them as they did so.

While I tuned into half-naked models lassoing bad guys, strong women who exhibited traits that were not traditionally "ladylike" were not approved by my grandmother. Women who questioned authority, were abrupt, or directly asserted themselves were hard for my grandmother to relate to. In fact, girls and women who did such forthright things were referred to as acting "the Margaret Thatcher way," not at all emulating the "be seen and not heard" tradition of my grandparents' homeland.

In the early days of my career, my grandmother used to ask me, "When are you going to stop being so ambitious and learn how to calm down so that a good man can find you?" I would smile and do my best to give her a pleasing answer because I knew I could not change her "pink perception." Girls *should be* nice, frilly; they *should be* liked, *should be* agreeable, and possibly *should* earn money by answering phones or fetching coffee for a *man*-ager in charge. I'd attempt to normalize her expectations of being prim and proper, appease her idea of having a "woman's job," like a secretary or nurse or other "support roles," and generally stayed quiet if I felt my needs were not met so as to not rock the boat that I was not captain of. But no matter how hard I tried to fall in line, I found myself torn between how I was being raised and what I felt I could achieve in life as a contemporary American woman—money, power, influence.

When I was around 10 years old, I began to live a double life as a way to silently feed the high-achieving hear-me-roar drive within while allowing my grandparents to believe I would follow our cultural traditions. While I acted politely and never complained to our neighbors, teachers, and elders, I tried on for size some really interesting alter egos. With a hairbrush microphone in hand, I'd command my imaginary audience in the bathroom mirror, sometimes open for Janet Jackson at Madison Square Garden, and produce a talk show that beat Oprah's ratings. While I strived for my grandmother's approval, I couldn't settle for her version of happiness, which was to find a husband, have children, and build security.

When I entered my career life, this double personality caused me to doubt myself at work because I felt like an imposter there, too. I was a fraud every which way I turned: At home, I wanted to be setting sail for the Manhattan skyline on the bow of the Staten Island Ferry while the theme song to *Working Girl* played. At work, marriage and children were drilled into my head as a backup plan in case that "ambition thing" didn't work out.

When I look back on my grandparents' cultural norms, I realize that I am not alone and these norms are not something only taught by the Caribbean's elder generation. This double personality, total confusion, and imposter syndrome are drilled into more women from more cultures, generations, and traditions than you can imagine. While women have made impressive strides entering, rising, and leading in the workforce, they still find themselves opting out of the pipeline before they reach the C-suite. The guilt just keeps on giving. At some point, they think they *shouldn't* and they *can't*, until they communicate—most unwittingly—exactly those things to the decision makers who silently watch them.

I've listened to the TED Talks, read an endless number of books, and attended thousands of conferences, but the question remained: "Why aren't there more women in the C-suite?" I deconstructed some of the ineffectiveness of the "empowerment movement" for women and discovered some interesting truths: there are enough conferences and books that cheer women on, but never teach them how to close the gap between where they are and the C-suite. The more I engaged in conversations about this discrepancy, it became clear that women are ambivalent about communicating with confidence, self-respect, and authority. It's the story of our lives. Raise your hand if you have ever . . .

- Knocked on doors politely and apologetically entering the room to go into a meeting
- Delayed an important conversation with your HR manager because you were waiting for the "right time" to ask for a well-deserved raise and promotion
- Raised your hand to add value in a meeting and asked for your turn in a childish manner
- Explained why you couldn't participate in the office softball game so your coworkers wouldn't dismiss you as a team player
- Stayed late or worked on a project that was not going to give you a chance at a promotion or pay increase
- Failed to brag about your accomplishments publicly and consistently, or played them down
- Giggled, fidgeted, or slouched when nervously confronting someone
- Felt intimidated by successful people
- Changed the tone of your voice to sound more pleasing and "ladylike," i.e., nonaggressive
- Created invisible milestones at work, such as, "When I get X, then they will give me Y."
- Kept your head down and worked hard, with the hope that someday, a decision maker will notice
- Compared yourself to others
- Described yourself generically, using nondescript adjectives and very little tangible evidence of your track record
- Discussed your inability to stay late in lieu of your family or parental obligations

All of the above are how women create limitations by explaining themselves too much, playing themselves small, and not communicating their value to those who need to know about it. But we will start with just the obvious—we just talk too much. Our communication strategy needs work, beginning with recognizing that we explain ourselves to feel normal and acceptable, all the while sabotaging the road to the C-suite. We have convinced ourselves that the world cares about—or is entitled to know—our reasoning behind the choices we make, and more importantly, has authority over them. As we begin to divulge irrelevant details about our personal lives and decisions ("I need to be home for my mother," "I've never done that task before," "I always get nervous when I speak"), we give away our power, underestimate ourselves, and nix opportunities for growth when we should be nabbing them. We show the decision makers we're *not* sure, we're *not* in charge, we *don't* know the road ahead. The joke is on us, because while we stutter things like, "I'm so sorry but," "yes, I can grab you coffee," or "Please forgive me, my child was up all night," we've already been judged, perceived. And the really important people tuned us out and moved on from the conversation—silently deeming us middle management at best.

On the other hand, men do not explain themselves, and nobody expects them to. They are brief and to-the-point without a level of guilt around the things that women obsess over in their attempt to over-justify themselves. Simply stated, men are conditioned to be direct, and women celebrate and reinforce that attribute. The pomp and circumstance of presenting any reasoning behind their decisions is simply not expected. We have normalized this expectation while complicating our own.

For instance:

- Men interrupt women in meetings unapologetically.
- Men apply for opportunities even if they're not 100 percent qualified for the position.
- Men do not apologize or knock softly when interrupting a meeting.
- Men do not raise their hands to add value in a meeting.
- Men speak up, even around the water cooler.
- Men highlight their accomplishments and achievements daily in a grandstanding way.
- Men don't spend their entire day apologizing for the simplest things such as being late to the office.
- Men expect a pay raise annually and advocate for themselves.
- Men say no without guilt while understanding that no is a full sentence.
- Men don't compare themselves to others, especially women.
- Men assess the cost-benefit analysis before volunteering for projects at work.
- Men are not invested in likability.
- Men are also not vulnerable to the opinions of others.
- Men are more likely to send out an email with misspellings and grammatical errors without an apology.

When I first founded and built The Confidence Factor for Women—an organization dedicated to helping more high-achieving women gain the confidence to enter and remain in the C-suite—I underestimated how much women unintentionally shrink themselves at work due to fear, guilt, and a feeling of inferiority and express the same defensiveness that I once felt. I have been in meetings where women have shared that they feel they cannot decline a project without explaining their decision, due to the fear of demotion or termination, unlike their male colleagues. They also feel bound by the pressure of motherhood and the enormous demands that are placed on them to find some level of balance between their personal life and their career expectations. I have heard the perils of women who feel like they have to explain every life interruption that impacts their professional journey, including childbirth, childcare, bereavement, marriage, divorce, or parental care. Women feel overwhelmed from the need to overcommunicate and explain every decision on top of the mounting issues regarding pay disparities, leadership opportunities and tracks, allyship, mentorship, and sponsorship. These factors continue to create a disconnect between the way men ask for promotions and how women feel ignored for the same opportunities.

Here is what I tell them: communication sets the standard for how the valuation for your expertise will be quantified. Effective communication is verbal (adding value in a team meeting) and nonverbal (creating a one-sheet of your deliverables); is always consistent; must reflect who you are and what standard you display, which is focused less on being liked and more on gaining respect. Although communication must never negate empathy and compassion (as lore would have it), you must be direct and intentional about the deliverable and expected goal.

The only thing that separates high-performance leaders from everyone else is their ability to communicate. It's what you say and how you say it—and sometimes what you don't say—that will help you gain access to life-changing opportunities. But, be clear: no explanation is required!

Don't blame yourself if you have not learned the communication skills you need. The educational system has not changed in my lifetime, and it is ineffective at teaching the skill of communicating and self-advocacy for the real world. Communication is a high-value skill that will give you access to very powerful rooms. I am living proof!

The first time I saw my name in *Forbes* magazine, it was the result of an informal conversation at Starbucks, not a pitch. I was at a Starbucks in Washington, DC, when the gentleman sitting beside me noticed I was listening to CNBC's *Squawk Box* on my iPad. I'm a Jim Cramer fan to the core, and he was discussing real estate investment trusts (REITs) and sharing the best trades. The gentleman asked, "Do you invest, or are you just a fan?" Rather than remaining dismissive or vague, I replied, "Yes, but I only allow my financial advisor to navigate my portfolio. They only sell the options they have and rarely give me any alternate advice."

He noticed my knowledge of the market and many intermediaries to help grow my investments. We had an hour-long conversation about trading, the stock market, and REITs. As he stood up to leave, he said, "You know, I write about this kind of stuff on my blog. Do you mind sharing your email just in case I am looking for experts for some content?"

"Sure!" I replied.

He never said he was a writer for *Forbes*; I thought he had a blog on Medium or Tumblr. A few days later, I was notified by *Forbes* that the magazine wanted to authenticate a quote, and the next morning, my name was mentioned on the platform. That five-line shout-out immediately increased my demand and value, and one thing led to another; soon people started asking me for the name of my publicist or a sample pitch letter for *Forbes*, neither of which I had.

Most of the world's highest-level executives have networked themselves from one opportunity to the other, while everyone else is writing their skills in chronological order on a résumé and hoping that this piece of paper in the perfect format will get them to the C-suite. Nothing could be further from the truth, because if you cannot sell yourself when you get to the room, the decision makers know the difference between something that was professionally written, versus the person who has the personality to show their qualifications. Do you think leaders such as Steve Jobs, Meg Whitman, or Elon Musk ever depended on a résumé? They networked their way to the C-suite—and so can you.

The definition of *network* is "to meet and talk to people in order to receive or give information, especially about business opportunities." You have to know how to talk if you are going to network. You must know how to receive and give information, verbally or nonverbally, if you are to send the right signals to the right people. The opportunity that changed my life was also my first real experience with the power of a network and the importance of communicating when navigating upward within it. My political science professor at Long Island University, Dr. Eric Lopez, said, "There's an opportunity for an internship at the Brooklyn District Attorney's office, and I think you are one of the best candidates for it." He went on to say, "I've arranged an appointment for you for tomorrow, so wear your best and bring your résumé."

Ah, a résumé—the one thing I didn't have, nor did I have time to draft one because I had a paper due the next morning. Besides, what was I going to put on it? "I am a lifelong academic with no professional experience and a 3.8 GPA?" Was that going to help me get this opportunity? Instead, I wore my best blue linen suit, gathered my high school and college transcripts, and hoped for the best. "Hope" was my nickname after all!

I was greeted by Selma Jackson, who is partially responsible for who I am today. She was the attorney in charge of assigning cases for discovery and obtaining witness statements. She was a sharp thinker, so my transcripts were not going to work on her. I shifted my strategy to a "become the candidate" approach, by listening to the description of duties she outlined during the interview and matching my "potential" talent to each task. I sat in her office and listened to her talk about her mother, her faith, and the fact that she had attended my alma mater. More importantly, I was listening to the cues that told me the kind of person I needed to be if I were to be considered the perfect candidate. In other words, I meticulously took notes and used her words to define how I responded. I allowed her to navigate the interview, but my answers reflected the candidate that she was describing. Selma gave me the internship the same day. It was my first corporate opportunity, and it had a residual lifelong effect.

Selma allowed me to go into some uncomfortable rooms with a few brilliant but shrewd prosecutors and arrogant judges in New York City. She taught me how to overcome my insecurities when working with the New York City Police Department, which, at that time, was completely headed by old white men. It was important to build alliances with the police department to move high-profile cases through the system with haste. There were so many times I just wanted to quit this internship because every day presented a new challenge that forced me to have a harsh exterior. There were moments when some of the judges and other prosecutors made me feel invisible and valueless just by their demeanor when I entered their offices. But Selma continued to push me harder and harder to go into bigger and tougher rooms and use my voice as the advocate for voiceless victims of violence in New York City.

By the end of the internship, I realized that I had gained a group of mentors who were vested in my success. The experience also led me to my next opportunity, which was a paralegal position in the private sector. Selma put in a great word for me, and a few of the prosecutors also wrote letters of recommendation for law school for me even before I sat the LSAT. From time to time, when I was in the downtown Brooklyn area, I would let a few of my favorite prosecutors and judges know ahead of time and invite them to lunch. Eventually, I realized that behind their tough demeanors were kind and compassionate people; I learned how to separate our workplace communication from our personal conversations. Even though I had left the public sector for the private sector, I continued to invest in those relationships. As I continued to climb the corporate ladder, I was not bound by a résumé; I had a network. Someone would put in a good word for me, I would show up to an interview—or what others like to refer to as an "exploratory conversation"—and the next thing I knew, I was hired!

The higher I went, however, the more masculine, and, in turn, lonelier work became.

How I Came to Write This Book

Years later, right before my final exit from corporate America, I had a job as a senior paralegal in a medical malpractice law firm. At the time, I was dating my now-husband, and he worked in the area. One day one of the male office managers made a joke, "It looks like you're pretty serious with that guy. Please don't get pregnant because we don't know how to fill out the maternity leave forms." That was my turning point. I went from having an unlimited supply of confidence to finding myself becoming defensive. I was in my late twenties, and the idea of settling down and having a family was something that I was deeply considering. However, I had never understood that most of the leverage I'd gained at work was because I was a single woman who could navigate her way around from one function to the other. The moment I let my guard down and shared some level of my personal life in public, I was vulnerable to harsh criticisms about gender expectations and the limitations of romance and motherhood.

During that time, my now-husband and I were already talking about marriage, and I realized that the idea of familial commitment is a separate stigma. I also found out the hard way that employers ask different questions of women in interviews than of men, especially if they are between the ages of 25 and 32. All the confidence I had built up until this moment was about to crumble under the weight and the gravity of the idea that marriage and children could impact my value. In the end, I chose my family and left corporate America to continue to address that stigma from an external perspective.

I did not know how I was going to make it on my own, without the cushion that corporate America provides, but I knew that I had the gift of salesmanship and I could sell my talent effectively, which is why I tossed my last résumé in the garbage almost 20 years ago. The best résumé I own is myself. I'm a walking and talking curriculum vitae, and

I can highlight my accomplishments at any moment, which a well-written CV cannot do. Now, I help women all over the world do the same through The Confidence Factor for Women. My company has been my platform to work with high-performance leaders to give them an external perception on their blind spots, promotion considerations, and how they are placing some of their best leaders in gender boxes and creating stereotypical expectations for women.

You Can Learn to Communicate Your Worth

Perception is everything in business and in how we communicate in our relationships. It's how we understand ourselves, how others interpret our strengths and abilities, and informs the mental impression we form about the future of work and the role we want to take within it. This conversation is especially important today, as we reimagine a post-Covid-19 workplace, with potential hybrid models and flexible options. The pandemic and the lockdowns that followed changed the way we relate to one another, how we dress, lead meetings, participate in virtual conversations, carry ourselves, use social media, give and take cues, and set boundaries. In fact, the sensitivities, intricacies, and misuse of communication have never been more prevalent and more at the forefront of how we do business and achieve our C-suite goals than it is today.

As a direct result of the pandemic, the way we communicate has transformed. Today, we must speak with a level of clarity and factor our mental health and well-being into our decisions. In a post-Covid-19 C-suite, it's imperative to consider if you are reactive or responsive under pressure. Before the pandemic, both styles were effective, but today, a responsive approach is necessary, which requires you to deliberate before reacting in haste. Also, it gives you a moment to assess if a response is necessary.

High-level leaders are great communicators who know the importance of deliberating and responding with a well-thought-out statement, rather than reacting impulsively. Reacting is an emotional response, and during this time, some people are more emotionally vulnerable. I've had to change my sharp-and-direct approach with my team in consideration of their needs and challenges. We are more mindful now, which has helped all of us understand each other better.

Regardless of which side of the pandemic you're on, remote work will no longer just be an option for a chosen few. However, even if you're not in the office, you must remain an important part of the office.

The mission of this book is to help bridge the self-promotion gap women experience that keeps them hidden in plain sight from the C-suite. We will do this by uncovering the insidious bad habit women have regarding how they speak and present themselves to the world: passiveness. Passive communication entails a plethora of actions, behaviors, tones, and words that will be addressed and reversed throughout the chapters of this book. You are too valuable to be invisible. By the end of this book you will know big things and little things that when put together amount to you becoming your own walking talking curriculum vitae.

With the advice, tools, and insights I will share, you will never Zoom again without turning your camera on and speaking up. When working in the office two days per week, you'll know how to make your presence known by adding value and becoming an outspoken leader. You don't need five days in a row to gather the attention of people with influence. You'll never again find yourself explaining your decisions to people who don't care and don't have the right or need to know what informs your choices. When asked an uncomfortable favor or given an unsolicited task, you'll know how to decline with aplomb unapologetically. You'll call people out on inappropriate comments. You will never again rattle on and on offering facts that are not germane to the conversation or reveal your personal life. You'll no longer focus on the popular response, but on the one that will provide you progress. Your mantra will be: *No Explanation Required!*

I used to believe that being "nice" and "likable" was my ticket into the C-suite, but after living for years without clear boundaries, I finally put my success on cruise control when I learned how to say no without explaining why. Heck, now I say yes and maybe without explaining why! It's such a liberating feeling, and today, clarity is key, not just for your decisions, but when you ask for what you deserve.

I am still a work in progress. There are moments when I hear my grandmother's voice reminding me to "be seen and not heard" or to "be happy to just have a job and a paycheck" or "you can always find a nice man and settle down." But I remind myself that I am hope. Amplifying my voice and exercising self-advocacy have catapulted me to the top of my game. They've turned me from likable to respectable, from passive to active, and from reactive to responsive. It took trial and error and a lot of talking myself off the ledge, but I promise, once you find the words, as you will through this book, you will find your worth—and know how to tell the world all about it!

1

The Self-Promotion Gap!
Creating a Winning Perception

I am not a pastry person. I enjoy a good chocolate chip cookie here and there, but I'm not someone who craves cake or other baked goods. Sweets have never been my weakness, until I spoke at an event in Chicago. The coordinator came into my dressing room with a tray of small cakes and finger sandwiches, and I indulged. When I bit into the cake, the velvety softness changed my life. I asked the coordinator which restaurant catered the cake. She pointed to the gentleman in the hallway and said, "He's the chef that prepared everything for today."

Like a lifelong fan, I introduced myself and told him that it was possibly the best cake I'd ever had. Full disclaimer: my grandmother was a professional pastry caterer for 20 years, and this was better than anything I'd ever tasted before. We spoke for a moment, and he told me that if I was ever in the Indianapolis area, I must come by his restaurant, but that he delivers across the country. When I came off stage, he was gone.

Two months later, he was the caterer for another event. We made eye contact and he remembered me, and we started to joke about the cake. I was fascinated (but not surprised) by how many event planners knew of this particular chef and why they all hired him.

"My cake was featured on a list of Oprah's Favorite Things back in the 1990s," he told me. Then it clicked, the *Oprah Effect*. Although he deserved every national acclaim he had earned, his feature on Oprah was over 20 years prior. When I looked at his T-shirt, which featured the name of his bakery and contact information, the back said, "As seen on The Oprah Show." Decades later, this chef was still using Oprah's famous television logo to brand himself. Some people might consider that living in the past, but he used it as leverage to create a perception in the outside world. His advice never left me: "Your accomplishments never expire until you stop talking about them."

It all made sense. It was his biggest media feature, and although it was long past, he still bragged about it as if it had happened yesterday. That level of pride opened up so many doors that he was able to expand his bakery into 217 more grocery locations over 20 years since his appearance on the show. There's nothing to be ashamed of when you have worked so hard to accomplish something meaningful. If you stop sharing it with the world, no one is going to ask you what you have accomplished.

On the flight home I thought about my own sense of pride in my accomplishments. Sadly, until I gave my first

TED Talk in 2015, I did not feel my measure of success mattered.

That line kept spinning around in my mind: "Your accomplishments never expire until you stop talking about them." I thought about all of the accomplishments that I've labored for but I've stopped sharing with the world out of shame because I had not done the next thing immediately after the last thing. I was worried about the relevance of every accomplishment and how to monetize something that I considered old, when in fact it had not expired at all. I thought I should begin bragging about myself and grabbed my notebook and started a bulleted list. *What have I done over the past decade? What small wins did I have that led to bigger ones? Why on earth am I not bragging about them?* And the facts of my career came pouring out of me:

- Shared the stage with Kevin O'Leary and Sara Blakely as a keynote speaker at an *Inc.* magazine event and ended up having dinner with the *Shark Tank* celebrity investor and several media producers after the event.
- Interviewed Wendy Williams about the power of negotiating and asking for what you deserve on the tenth anniversary of her hit talk show, *The Wendy Williams Show.*
- Sat down and had a conversation with Barbara Corcoran of *Shark Tank* and asked her how she turned $1,000 into the $66 million empire that still holds her name.
- Interviewed Ryan Serhant of the hit Bravo show *Million Dollar Listing New York* about how to build a successful brand after he launched his YouTube channel and second book.

- Spoke at Facebook's Women@ Leadership Day in San Francisco. (When I walked off the stage I was greeted by Sheryl Sandberg and Jada Pinkett Smith, who were watching my speech from the greenroom in amazement. Sheryl Sandberg made me tea to help me recover my voice after that talk, and it was such an amazing moment to be celebrated by such an inspiring soul.)
- Addressed Harvard Business School and Columbia Business School on women in leadership to groups of some of the finest and most brilliant women who are still changing the world today.
- Was a guest on *The Steve Harvey Show*, where I discussed *The Balancing Act* and its impact on mothers. (That eight-minute segment took almost an hour to film, as Steve Harvey can keep you laughing for days while inspiring you to continue to push forward.)
- Was a guest on *The Today Show* due to a piece that I published in *Forbes* titled "Why Don't More Women Negotiate?" (I remember the morning that the producer from the show called me to tell me that my article popped up on her feed and she thought it was a great direction to take the show that day during Women's History Month. I filmed that episode only a few days after my father's funeral.)
- Was a guest on the first pilot episode of *On Your Side Tonight with Jamie Boll*. (Jamie Boll is a locally famous news anchor, who hosts a talk show based on current events before the start of Covid-19; it was an honor to sit next to a local legend, especially on his first show, while discussing diversity and inclusion for women.)

- Am a writer for *Inc.* and *Entrepreneur* and have been featured by both magazines for my work with women and negotiating.
- Spoke about Women and Confidence on the acclaimed TEDx stage. (It was a moment that brought tears to my eyes—sometimes I still pinch myself when people tag me on social media about my talk.)
- Received honorable mentions in *Forbes, Inc., Entrepreneur, Glamour,* the *Wall Street Journal,* and other periodicals.
- Had my advice featured in so many books that I stopped counting.
- Had my name appear in academic white papers and other published works in different languages around the world.

I believe every meeting in life has a divine purpose. Meeting the caterer allowed me to see that bragging is not negative at all. I had the wrong approach and wrong thinking about what it meant to be proud. My encounter with the caterer helped me to see that the moment you begin to discount your accomplishments, your verbiage and communication style can diminish the value of the accomplishment. The caterer never discounted his *Oprah* appearance or downgraded it with the passing of time. He never said, "I appeared a long time ago on a talk show" and labeled it as just a chance meeting. He was intentional and boastful.

After filming my appearance on *The Steve Harvey Show* in 2013, on the flight home I stared out the window and imagined how displeased my grandmother would have been to hear me bragging about my success to a world-famous comedian on national television. I cried tears of joy and tears of fear for the entire two-hour flight. I knew that if I wanted to change the trajectory of my family for future generations, I had to trust my instinct and stop playing it small; stop being the modest female and the nice girl who doesn't brag about the great things she has done. I wanted the world to perceive me as someone worth listening to and partnering with, so I needed to be more demonstrative.

Almost a year after the show aired, I continued to wrestle with the idea that the accomplishment of appearing on a panel segment on Steve Harvey's show was no longer relevant; it was in the past, and when it comes to the media, nobody has a memory. So, I removed it from my curriculum vitae (CV) and press kit. At times, I listened to the limiting beliefs that made me self-sabotage my greatness. The words of the caterer replaying in my mind led me to revive the 2013 appearance on all of my marketing materials. The moment I reshared my segment on Steve Harvey's show, other media outlets began to call and ask me to discuss issues of gender diversity. Subsequently, that's how I landed on the evening news, which led to much more. The ripple effect would not have been possible had I not encountered the caterer who was consistently sharing his good news with the world for over two decades.

What's Bragging Got to Do with It?

Bragging is one of the most valuable forms of communication. You don't need to have the influence of Oprah to start sharing your brilliance with the world. It is not the blatant act of grandstanding and gloating that you may think. It is the act of highlighting your best qualities and highest performance skills by using your own proven results, experiences, and expertise. Think of it as the highlight reel of your professional and personal achievements. It opens doors and will give you access to high-level meetings and professional opportunities in a way that your résumé cannot. The key to using bragging as a communication strategy is that you must be consistent and immediate. Bragging will catch the attention of decision makers, and it may be a little overload for your colleagues, but remember your objective is professional ascension, not friendships. Bragging has a negative connotation in social settings, but if you are highly ambitious, it is pivotal in your communication style. Bragging is about overcommunicating proven results and narrating your experiences with confidence and clarity. It helps form responses that are well-thought-out, powerful, and unwavering. Owning your accomplishments and communicating them is the opposite of being passive—one of the stereotypes we must always be aware of—along our career trajectory.

Perhaps you've been debating whether you should apply for the senior-level leadership opportunity recently posted at your company. Maybe you've been wishing to get out of middle management and updating your CV to put your hat in the ring, but you are afraid of rejection, so you debate and procrastinate.

You may be more qualified for that senior-level role than you give yourself credit for. Because you do not brag enough about what you have done for your company or firm thus far, other people will fail to give you credit as well. You negate your accomplishments by talking about the "team's" success rather than about your leadership style that directs the team toward its success. By limiting your role as the leader of the team, you have negated your ability to lead a team. It is easy to see how a small communication error can make the difference between getting the role you want versus being passed over for a promotion.

Bragging is a career and business game changer. I have used it many times throughout my professional journey to continue to get into specific rooms, especially when I knew that I was more than qualified. In my law firm life, I used it during evaluations to get a raise that was worthy of my expertise, especially when I continued to prove that my relationship-building skills brought in tens of millions of dollars in new business and publicity for the firm. Speaking in first person and narrating my achievements helped the decision maker understand that I was the clear leader on the team. As much as we frown upon bragging, you will lose valuable opportunities by conveying your value in second and third person. Speak about you and only you. It is not selfish—it creates a focal point in the decision-making process. Focus on you!

Don't be afraid to come across as a know-it-all or a grandstander—it is a welcomed attribute as a leader. It will work to your benefit to speak of your accomplishments. Decision makers will realize they have an asset within their company. Stop remaining the "best-kept secret" at work. Bragging is not an aspirational form of communication, but rather an effective tool to ensure decision makers are aware of who contributes exceptional value and exemplifies leadership potential. You will come to understand that bragging is the best communication tool to lead you to the next opportunity.

If I didn't brag about my ability to book myself as a guest on *The Steve Harvey Show*, I would not have received an offer to be on the *Today* show. If I did not show my communication style and capabilities on blogs such as Tumblr or Medium, I would not have had the opportunity to write for *Forbes, Entrepreneur,* or *Inc.* magazines. If I did not show my ability to solve a problem within the world of diversity and inclusion for women, *O, The Oprah Magazine* wouldn't have interviewed me for a recent article. If I did not prove my ability to speak in front of 10 people, I would not have been invited to speak to an audience of 100,000. Every boastful "brag" that I've shared has led to the next opportunity, which has increased my value significantly. I've used bragging as a communication tool to allow others to see what I have accomplished in the past and assess how they're going to place my expertise within their company in the future. Bragging is currency, and you have to use it every day to open up a multitude of opportunities.

I know you may be scratching your head, thinking, "Bragging is the new form of currency?" But think about it for a moment: Have you ever wanted to purchase something on Amazon, but were skeptical about the quality until you read the reviews? People who have already purchased the product validate your choice, simply because they shared their experience. Subsequently, the product rises in rank on Amazon, and the seller has the option to raise the price due to demand. This is why bragging is a new form of currency. Amazon sellers post their stellar reviews on other platforms to continue to increase sales and the value of their brand.

Bragging is not selfish. We must change that stigma. Besides, when you don't brag, you are leaving money on the table. Meanwhile, your colleagues and competitors are swiftly moving ahead of you—not due to education, but due to the megaphone they use daily to make others pay attention.

Throughout this book, I'm going to continuously remind you to be clear, confident, and conscious with your words—using everyday vocabulary. It is your job, no one else's, to articulate your value. People do not judge you on your intention, they judge you based on your words—words you are completely responsible and accountable for; words that brag about who you are. Finding the confidence to articulate yourself requires consistent application, so be patient with yourself as you emerge out of conditioned ways of communicating and thinking. Now is the time to focus on your professional growth. You're going to have many slips and triggers that may cause you to regress, but the one thing I'm committed to is helping you change your passive voice.

Be loud and proud. Highlight your education, accreditations, and leadership skills; declare your desired career path within the company, relationships, and references; and make known any other information that is essential for decision makers to know about your commitment to accelerate as a leader within your career. Your desire for growth must be greater than your fear of what others may say about your level of confidence.

Is Your CV Holding You Back?

Before I left corporate America, I ripped up the last résumé I drafted because I realized it was ineffective at helping me secure the career of my dreams. My résumé kept me stuck in a cycle of settling for "jobs" that were similar to the last "job" listed there. Instead of ascending in my career, I was moving in a horizontal line, with no executive presence or new challenges to show. I felt like

I was trapped on a merry-go-round. I tried to make my résumé "pretty" and scripted, tried to say all the right things, strike the "right" chords, which meant playing it small, not bragging at all, focusing on fancy words with no context, and making myself a template. I embellished my vocabulary on a document, but then minimized myself in person.

Throughout my journey over the last 10 years as a keynote speaker for some of the biggest corporations in the world, including Facebook, *Inc.*, TEDx, and more, I've found this dependency on a résumé to be universal. Every time I come off a stage, audience members ask, "What do I say? Do you know where I can find a template?" They are always looking for the best way to draft the perfect CV or LinkedIn summary for a tenured track to executive-level leadership opportunity. Many of them reference the education, certifications, references, referrals, and powerful CV they have, but still feel like the C-suite is unattainable. They are hiding behind a template to do all of the talking.

I replaced my résumé with a document called a One Sheet. Professional speakers and performers use a similar format to get hired or booked for appearances. A One Sheet is a document that focuses on your highest-level skills, with verifiable testimonials, and lists other skills or topics that you are available to explore. A One Sheet is not in chronological order, and the goal is to only discuss your high-value skills, talents, and achievements. One of the first accomplishments I used on my One Sheet was: "I helped win an $8,000,000 settlement for my law firm, which was the first multimillion-dollar settlement for a claimant under 10 years old in Nassau County, NY. I am available to discuss with you in detail my formula during our exploratory meeting."

I knew that the only way to get high-level opportunities or to that highly desired "seat at the table" would require me to talk my way into rooms that made me uncomfortable and oftentimes scared. Besides, people give opportunities to people in their network or to those who can demonstrate their value, not solely using a professionally crafted résumé, but by knowing the art of the brag.

The Self-Promotion Gap

A *U.S. News* study stated, "Another drawback of failing to share your accomplishments is that it can hold you back at work. If your supervisor, colleagues, and other team members aren't aware of your capabilities and past experiences, you may get passed over for career opportunities."

In other words, if you don't speak up, you will be overlooked. We often suffer in silence and communicate with fear when the spotlight is on us. We practice, and practice, and practice until we have perfected what we want to say, but when the moment comes, our posture changes and we become reluctant to speak. Instead of highlighting our potential, we start a sentence with "I think," which highlights our insecurities.

Imagine if a heart surgeon came up to you and said "I think" you need heart surgery, rather than stating, "The left ventricle needs to be repaired based on the echocardiogram we saw this morning." "I think" implies a hypothesis of maybe you can or maybe you can't. It does not imply a level of confidence about your ability to complete the task. Although you are not intentionally trying to diminish the conversation or the thought, you are communicating doubt. This could be the difference between a promotion and a demotion based on how you communicate your successes, previous wins, and accomplishments.

The thesis of The Self-Promotion Gap, a survey commissioned by Mighty Forces, Southpaw Insights, Upstream Analysis, and Grey Horse Communications in January 2019, is based on a study of 1,016 participants, both men and women, in which 69 percent of women stated they would rather diminish or minimize their accomplishments in public. It expresses the fact that women simply "undersell their accomplishments, thereby minimizing their impact." Another factor that contributes to this disparity in self-promotion and bragging is race, ethnicity, and age. When you have the issue of competitive alienation, coupled with race and ageism, it leaves an imbalance in how women of one age spectrum may appear more confident than others of another age spectrum. I have felt this level of disparity, especially when my family conditioned me to believe that bragging was a negative thing, but I knew I needed it to succeed in the real world.

I was asked to join a board of directors for a public company. I attended the exploratory session to see if I was the best fit for the association. I walked into a room of 35 people, mostly men over the age of 65. There was another woman behind me who was also up for the same consideration. We both attended the meeting with a bit of optimism that we could change the old boys club, but we were wrong.

The president of the association was possibly in his early- to mid-seventies, handsome, tall, with a very distinct baritone voice. Of the 35 people in attendance, there were maybe two or three women. The president of the association started the meeting. He was polite and accommodating to all of the board members who had invited guests to explore this opportunity. He took a moment to congratulate us on our presence, and then the meeting began.

The organization was exploring marketing efforts to begin a diversity campaign to attract younger customers, primarily millennials. The other woman who joined me in this exploratory consideration asked for a moment to speak to the group.

"I think what you should do is purchase a few Facebook ads and . . ."

Before she could finish her sentence, the president stood up and said, "Ma'am, you're here for an exploratory consideration, not to contribute any ideas. The best thing you can do is sit down and let the pros run this organization from here."

Every member in the room turned their head to see to whom he was speaking. The woman sat quietly in the back of the room, cowering. Instead of announcing that she was a former marketing executive for Jet.com, which was subsequently purchased by Amazon for $3 billion, and that she knew about marketing, she fell into a submissive role. The abrupt interruption of her voice dismissed her qualifications, as that president refused to allow her to speak.

I felt like I was in elementary school, and the principal was walking around so we had to behave. I will admit, I could have been an advocate for her, and as I look back, I should have spoken up. At that moment, however, I froze because I was worried that if I defended her, I could lose my consideration for this opportunity. We must stop using the repetitive excuse of getting in the door or getting a seat at the table to justify our silence. Most women take a back seat when they are interrupted at work instead of speaking up about all the things they have done and are qualified to do in their new or potential roles.

She didn't speak up and state her qualifications. It was her ability to market Jet.com that had led to Amazon's interest in taking over the popular app. Instead of starting the sentence with, "I'm a former marketing executive for Jet .com, which will soon be purchased by Amazon, and I can help you through this marketing agenda," she commenced her statement with "I think," which is a passive way of publicly casting doubt.

In my experience, I've seen the fear of alienation as a driving factor for women who play themselves small. The more I have accomplished, the more acquaintances and colleagues I've lost along my journey. I have been called every name you can imagine by people who I considered friends. Pride in oneself casts a stigma, especially in the eyes of other women. We are nurturers by nature and want the best for everyone, even if that means sacrificing our dreams for the good of others.

I was determined to continue my journey—regardless of whether my friends and colleagues supported my bravery or not—to bet on myself. The way I see it, life is too short to be scared of the opinions of others, to dictate our behaviors and words to be likable. I have never been driven by ego, but I am a highly determined person with ambition. Shining my light has worked very well for me, and it can be the same for you.

No matter where you go, you have to openly pat yourself on the back. No one is going to pat you on the back quite like you can. You have to give yourself more credit for your successes, past and present, and even those successes you will have in the future. Your next opportunity is a direct result of your ability today to celebrate how far you've come while allowing others to understand your value beyond.

Learning the Art of the Brag

According to Walter E. Jacobson, MD, psychiatrist and author of *Forgive to Win!*, our subconscious mind plays a major role in the actualization of our lives and the manifestation of our desires. What we believe about ourselves at a subconscious level can have a significant impact on the outcome of events.

I believe that fear is directly connected to the inability to affirm ourselves and our greatness. Instead, we subject ourselves to a level of habitual diminishing and dismissive association with our past. It is essential to develop a self-affirmation routine to become an effective communicator first to yourself and then to others. Think of instances in the past, when someone may have complimented you, either at work or walking down the street, and you refused to own it. Rather, you dismiss it as "Glad to help," or "I just want what's best for you" or "That's nothing, don't make a big deal of it."

You dismiss the achievement and are less likely to share it with others.

Here are some ways to practice the art of the brag:

- **Make good use of bragging and self-promotion.** Remember that bragging is a form of communication that highlights your achievements and accomplishments. Do not use it as a competitive tool to dismiss or discount the contributions of others on your team or your colleagues. Use it in a positive way to continue to provide relevant examples of your previous experiences that are germane to the opportunity you deserve. You've done the work, now share it in high-level circles.

- **Speak in first person.** If you work in a team environment, avoid the impulse to give the entire team credit for your leadership abilities. Your career depends on you to narrate your own story and take credit for your contributions. However, you can lose your moment to shine your highlight reel and promote yourself if you forget to mention "I" in your conversations with decision makers. Remember, you want a seat at the table, not the team. It is not selfish to only mention yourself and give yourself praise for an exceptional work product and result. Speak about you and only you.

- **Share your own reviews.** Major retailers such as Amazon and Best Buy post customer reviews of their high-ticket items. It is a way to gain access to repeat customers and helps with brand awareness. Your work is your brand. When you are praised for your results, or receive a great review, make sure you share it with others. Nothing is worse than becoming the best-kept secret in the office when there are empty chairs in the C-suite. Brag about what others say about your performance as well. Those who can substantiate your performance will accelerate your journey. Also, add it to your CV.

- **Make your accomplishments last a lifetime!** Bragging is not date sensitive. Whether you did something great four days ago or 40 years ago, it is still worthy of sharing. Stop thinking about *when* the accomplishment happened, and focus on the *value* of the achievement itself. It is worthy of sharing for a lifetime and part of your CV. "Your accomplishments never expire until you stop talking about them."

- **Brag to win the next opportunity.** As stated, I've used the last opportunity to attract the next opportunity, and all of it is thanks to bragging. Don't use this communication tool maliciously; rather use it as a magnet to attract new relationships, allyship, sponsors, and off-market opportunities for professional growth.

- **Be consistent!** I will repeat this throughout the book. Most people try something only once and give up. This is your story, and you must share it consistently. It is the only way to ensure all of the decision makers who are in a gatekeeping capacity will learn about who you are and the value you can add to another opportunity. Keep in mind that most decisions about promotions and the candidates that are being vetted happen when you are not in the room, or even in the office. It's important to make your presence known.

What Is the Remunerative Value for Your Skills?

In my negotiation workshops and training I discuss the importance of knowing your replacement and remunerative values. For example, I had a flood in my home in 2015. The insurance adjuster asked me for the "replacement" value of the items destroyed, and the claims department asked for the "remunerative" value for the same items.

The replacement value considers the items as a loss, and the remunerative value is based on the current value of the item, such as a television, tools, or a washing machine, factoring in the cost of inflation since it was purchased and the increased price over time of similar items due to demand.

Your remunerative value at work is based on how much you have increased the value of your team, department, or role during your tenure. More importantly, it factors in the cost of inflation, which I refer to as your increased value. Your value continues to increase with training, events, and new skills. When you list your skills and achievements in a negotiation meeting, commence the conversation with the amount of value or revenue you have brought in during your tenure in your current role, then think about how much your contribution is worth.

Here is an example of how to develop your remunerative value statement.

*During my tenure as sales director **(skill)**, I have increased revenue by 64 percent and closed more than $18 million in sales **(achievement)**. Effectively, due to performance, I believe the value of my role should increase by 22 percent **(remunerative value)**.*

Skill	
Achievement	
Remunerative Value	

What Is Your Remunerative Value Statement?

_____

_____

_____

_____

_____

_____

_____

_____

_____

_____

_____

2

Perception and Performance
Creating a Cycle of Professionalism

─────── KEY TAKEAWAY ───────
How people perceive you determines
how they interact with you.

When I first began hosting my live events and conferences for The Confidence Factor for Women, I was on a quest for guest speakers. I wanted to attract and host experts in various domains who would add value, breadth, and depth to my audience. One speaker, "Debbie," specialized in sales. After our initial conversation and an invitation to investigate her website credentials, she asked to meet me for lunch so we could explore further my event and how she might fit into my content.

For our lunch date, I chose to wear a bow-tie Gucci dress, a pair of classic black pumps, and a bag to match. I completed my look with nude lip gloss and a light dusting of face powder. It was important as I began to build and grow my network of speakers that I and my events be perceived as paramount. I was focused on the big time, and everything I did, said, and wore needed to reflect such an intention. I'd been a guest on *The Steve Harvey Show*, NPR, and the *Today* show by this time, and I felt I had a lot to offer speakers in terms of their brand extensions and believed I should look professionally consistent, just as I had on television.

I found Debbie sitting at a table by the bar. "Carol!" she yelled and waved me over, "Hey, you look great!" Except, I couldn't say the same for Debbie, who was wearing yoga pants with fuzzy slippers and an Old Navy T-shirt. With her hair in a fuzzy bun, she could've just popped over from the gym, and I felt instantly distracted. It was like agreeing to have a drink with someone you met online, only to find they looked *nothing* like their profile.

First impressions matter. The impression I wanted to give was that this event was significant to me and the women I serve. I wanted to ensure that I appeared as a leader, and less as a friend, especially since we were meeting for the first time. I reserve my casual look for the fifth and sixth meetings, not the first one. Also, I thought of this more as an interview, not specifically a job interview, but considering she was asking for $20,000+ to give a speech, I thought she should look the part. As she pitched me on her expertise, all I could think was how, no matter how much she spoke about her experience, I couldn't take her seriously. The more she continued to speak, the more I focused on how her lack of professionalism impacted my perception of her.

In a *Harvard Business Review* article titled "How to Give an Employee Feedback About Their Appearance" Amy Gallo writes "Whether we like it or not, a person's appearance affects their success at work." But still, I had to audit myself and check my own bias on the way home, thinking, *Carol, are you being judgmental? Did you give the wrong impression of the purpose of this meeting?* I doubted myself because my perception of what she had advertised on her website was different from the person who sat in front of me for lunch. She was also a bit arrogant and foul-mouthed and had very little filter, which caused me to have concern about how she would communicate unscripted if she were to interact with any conference attendees.

Later, her assistant sent a formalized commitment for her appearance, which was presumptuous as I had not hired her for the job. The email read:

> We typically require a hold agreement to block out a date. I see in [her] notes that she wants to prepare and deliver 3 hours of content for her typical hourly fee of $8,900. It says that you want a 1-hour keynote presentation then a subgroup 2-hour workshop. Is this accurate? It also says that she is waiting on you for attendee information to create an outline for the training.
>
> [She] says in her notes that you are "Awesome" :)
>
> Please let me know how you would like to arrange the training day as well (time/location) and I will prepare the hold agreement.

Very few people can say they make over $20,000 for three hours of their time, so I believed that the perception needed to match the reality. In the end, I could not bring myself to hire her for my event. I have never had to think that hard about a decision before, but I think I made the right one. As a leader, if I can't stand by the people I am hiring, then I would be wrong to introduce them as an expert to the people I am leading.

You will attract leadership opportunities only if you are perceived as a leader. Indeed, you will never get a second chance to make a first impression. In an article published on the website Well+Good, entitled "How Your Perception Is Your Reality, According to Psychologists," Jessica Estrada states "Perception is merely a lens or mindset from which we view people, events, and things." To reach the C-suite, the mindset has to be one of strength, professionalism, and talent, which is why perception is everywhere in the business world. If you want to be viewed as someone qualified and confident, you will prepare your appearance, your body language, and your language to not be self-limiting but to elevate interactions with decision makers.

If you walk around with your head down in the office, chances are you will be perceived as someone who is sad, depressed, lacking confidence, tired, or just not interested in your role. On the other hand, if you want to shift perception, walk with your head up—you'll be perceived as a leader, confident, strong, resilient, and engaged.

The perception we have of others, the perception others have of us, and the perception we have of ourselves are all within our control, if we have the right tools.

How People Perceive You

What you put out there is your decision alone. Debbie decided to wear workout clothes and a messy bun and to drop the f-bomb in order to get a $20,000 job. It turned out to be the wrong approach for Debbie, but it was still her choice. It's so much more than your appearance: perception is formed by the way you speak and the ways you interact with everyone around you. Communicating with perception in mind will lead to ensuring that decision makers trust you to take on responsibility and lead people.

Based on Debbie's appearance I perceived her as untrustworthy, disorganized, careless, and unenthused. I also believed that an investment in her did not match the interaction because the résumé outlined from her public profile did not match the person I met. Within the first five seconds, I made a judgment that this was not an equally matched opportunity. I also thought that she thought I was not important enough, or maybe she misinterpreted what a lunch meeting, emphasis on "meeting," required. Either way, she shaped my perception of her, not the other way around.

As a decision maker my biggest concern was how she would represent me and my company. Other decision makers around the world feel exactly the same. Would I endorse a person who came to our first meeting dressed with little intention? It's not the clothes that are the concern, but the lack of time and energy and focus shown in preparing to meet me. What else in her life did she prepare for haphazardly? Could I trust this person to represent my brand and my mission in alignment with the way I was building The Confidence Factor for Women? I couldn't take a risk that she would be the "talk" of the event, and not in a good way. I worried about the impression, or lack of impression, she would leave on my audience. If she did not perceive our first meeting to be of enough importance or significance to avoid wearing yoga pants to a lunch meeting that she solicited, then what could happen on the day of the event—an event I was taking the risk to finance? I was the decision maker in this scenario, and I couldn't take any chances. People perceive you by who you surround yourself with. In this case, I had worked hard to be the confident and competent businessperson, so I needed to be guaranteed that I'd be surrounded by leaders who also acted the part.

Based on Debbie's assistant's presumptuous correspondence with my office, it was clear Debbie didn't see herself the way I saw her. She saw herself as more than qualified, and maybe in the past, her appearance had worked for her in other meetings with other decision makers. That's because perception is subjective. What makes one person believe you to be a leader may be overlooked by another. A handshake might win someone over, while a person's close talking distance might turn someone else off. Because of the high subjectivity, you need to be more cautious than ever! One of my mentors said that the way you shake hands with people shapes their perception of you. He also told me that a strong handshake can be the difference between getting a seat at the table or being left out of the room. "Perception is the process of selecting, organizing, and interpreting information," according to a study by the University of Minnesota, "Communication in the Real World." "This process affects our communication because we respond to stimuli differently, whether they are objects or persons, based on how we perceive them."

The name of the game is to influence gatekeepers to talk positively about you when you are not in the room. If they do not trust you, do not think you planned in advance, or see you as not engaged or enthused about the business you are in, your name will never come up as a contender. When you have limited access to key people, as most people who are not in the C-suite do, perception needs to be leveraged so your name is brought up and their perception of your value is discussed. Decisions about promotions are not just based on your productivity but on the perception of your ability to handle the promotion. It is a never-ending cycle of perception and performance. Perception is a different form of currency at work that can only be shaped by you. Perception plays a key role in your professional ascension.

Perception and Self-Promotion

In her talk at the JCI Foundation in 2016, Carla Harris, vice-chairman and senior client advisor at Morgan Stanley, said "Perception is the co-pilot to reality. How people perceive you will directly impact how they deal with you and it's important [that] if you want to maximize your success you should understand the perception that exists about you in the marketplace. Remember that you can train people to think about you and the way that you want them to think about you."

We spoke at length in Chapter 1 about women's general lack of self-promotion in the workplace. Placing an emphasis on perception as you climb the corporate ladder is a reminder to keep talking yourself up. Shaping the narrative of how you want to be perceived within the workplace is a form of self-promotion. One strategy that sets up certain perceptions is to start a "rumor" about yourself. For example, I have started a rumor within my company that I make fast decisions. When members of my team or any outside stakeholders approach me with a project that needs an immediate decision, they always say, "Hey Carol, can you take a look at this for me real quick? I know you make fast decisions." I always say, "Yeah drop it off, let me take a look and I'll get back to you ASAP," which normally means the next morning. I am also selective in accepting projects, so it helps to work quickly, as I am careful with my time. I like to keep that perception going so that I have more stakeholders trusting me with high-profile projects. That's my secret rumor but I have created it around my brand.

Self-Perception

How we perceive ourselves matters more than how others perceive us. We must have a positive self-perception before we can put our best foot forward. What we believe about ourselves is what we exhibit to the world. If we perceive ourselves as less than others, we will certainly communicate that as a matter of fact.

I am always my own best and worst critic. I am constantly giving myself feedback so I remember to grow and add more opportunities while expanding my network. One of my strongest qualities is humor, and I enjoy making people laugh. My love of comedy comes across in my presentations and meetings. I recently received a call from one of my tenants on the day of her scheduled cesarean section, and when I answered I jokingly said "Aren't you busy today?" She laughed and replied, "I had the twins an hour ago, but I wanted to let you know that we mailed our rent payment this morning, just in case it's late."

Her call reinforced my leadership style. Immediately after a life-changing, monumental event, my tenant remained concerned about her fiduciary obligations. Most people would wait, but my humor mixed with firm leadership has helped me create a perception that I am approachable, with limitations. How you perceive yourself is a critical skill. As an investor, I need my tenants and other stakeholders to feel the same when I'm not in the room—"She's funny but firm."

Focus on the impression you want to leave on others and your leadership abilities. I ask myself after every meeting or event—"Did they think I was smart? Did I give them the best version of my knowledge, or did I dilute it? Did I come across as a leader today?" I also answer my questions so I can compare what I did well as opposed to what needs work.

PERCEPTION AND PERFORMANCE

Think about the impact you want to leave with others. Self-perception requires a self-assessment to ensure you gain the trust of decision makers while allowing them to observe the quality of your contribution. Look at yourself from their perspective. Also, ask yourself if you did your best today, and create a list of attributes that need your attention. This will allow you to attract opportunities instead of competing for them.

When I met Debbie for lunch, she changed my perception. I was sold from our phone conversation and her website, but I am still in the public figure business, so her public image shifted my perspective on hiring her. What I saw was someone who depended on her website image to attract opportunities. Perhaps she misinterpreted my humor during our conversation as a friendship rather than a working relationship. I also interpreted her approach in this meeting as a form of disrespect for a first impression. Although we live in a world where people continue to discount the significance of appearance, I assure you it is real. Those who live by this philosophy may not have your level of ambition and goals. Before you start thinking about Mark Zuckerberg and his famous gray T-shirt, consider his appearance when he is called before Congress. It may work for his business, but it doesn't work for everyone. You are always being judged. Even when I was in corporate America, I didn't participate often in "dress-down Fridays." I always thought of it as a science experiment—who was the worst dressed?

"Their" Perception

Perhaps your professional goals cannot be achieved at your current company, and you need to amicably part ways. How others perceive you can impact your transition to your next opportunity. It's not just how you perceive yourself and how others perceive you, you must also consider how others convey their perception of you and your strengths to others.

While I worked as an intern at the Brooklyn district attorney's office, I was aware that the opportunity was a launching pad for my future career. I worked diligently to ensure that everyone who I worked with, in any capacity, could relay the same experience of my professional candor to others. I was meticulous about creating a perception of dependability, excellence, and consistency because it was clear that the position was temporary. I took the internship seriously—from my clothes to volunteering for open assignments—I was aware of the rebound effect it could have in my life. Subsequently, "their" perception led me to private sector law firms and political networks, which have changed my life.

Create a perception that gatekeepers can convey to others, one that says you can do the job higher than where you are now. Your next opportunity to elevate your career is directly connected to someone putting in a referral or recommendation. How will they share their experiences and encounters with you? You must become mindful of anything nonverbal or verbal you might be doing that sends messages that you are limited to the role you are in and cannot handle more.

Avoiding Self-Limiting Language and Behaviors

The first time I pitched an idea and asked for $7.8 million, I was a nervous wreck. My lack of confidence reeked from my shrunken posture, shaky voice, and the deer-in-headlight expression on my face. I stood there, in front of a room of seven investors and two city planners from the Department of Housing and Urban Development, and I tried everything in my power to overcome my fear, but I just could not seem to get myself together. At the end of the meeting, I realized all my mistakes were in my language and posture. They sent cues that screamed, "She's not ready!" You can overcome nerves, and people can look past fear, but if your language is self-limiting, you will be perceived as underqualified.

When I walked into the pitch, I said:

*I'm a **new** investor who is interested in the $7.8 million grant that is offered by the Housing and Urban Development Redevelopment fund. I **think** I have a few ideas that could be of great use to the South End Neighborhood. I want to **try** to bring in a few more shops, and affordable houses.*

I bolded the words that caused the investors to shift their perception of my confidence level and abilities. If you read the same statement with the words in bold omitted, it could be perceived that I'm an experienced investor who has great ideas to share with the Housing and Urban Development Redevelopment fund. Those few small words that I used in front of that panel shifted their perception, and when I listened to my presentation afterward, I realized the flaw was my use of limiting language instead of using language to shift the perception.

Just as language can be powerful and help us avoid self-limitations, there are other behaviors and actions we can be purposeful about in order to put forth the best perception of ourselves and gain the trust and attention of decision makers:

Make eye contact. Eye contact is a form of nonverbal communication. Decision makers want to see that you can look them in the eye and trust you. AJ Harbinger published a *Business Insider* article entitled "7 Things Everyone Should Know About the Power of Eye Contact," which states, "If you want people to remember what you said long after you're done talking, maintain good eye contact . . . [it] makes people both more memorable and more noticeable."

Avoid wandering eyes in high-power meetings and presentations. Connect with decision makers so you can gain their trust. Looking them in the eye is the only way to change your perception about the type of leader you are capable of being. Shifty eyes, looking off in the distance, or staring or blinking too much can be seen as indicators that you are not trustworthy, not engaged, unfocused, or nervous.

Speak in the first person. Take ownership of all of your achievements in both written and verbal communication. Rather than starting a sentence with "They are," start with "I am." Self-promote and shine the spotlight on yourself, so you shift the perception from being one of many on a group project to being a team leader. It is so much more influential when you take ownership of your contributions and talents.

Communicating in the first person will help you to sound authentic and confident. It does not need to come across as arrogant. In fact, communicating in the first person can be an inclusive dialogue. For example:

We decided to cancel the event due to inclement weather.
(First-person plural)

They canceled the event due to inclement weather.
(Third person)

In the first example, you take ownership of your part on the team, instead of stating, "I canceled the event due to the inclement weather." Using "we" in the first person allows you to acknowledge yourself as a leading contributing member, without discounting the efforts of others, and highlight that you were part of the decision-making process. These are the kinds of statements that decision makers like to hear. You can interchange "I" and "we" numerous times but in a way that makes it clear that you were part of the decision-making process. This simple change will ensure that you are viewed more as an equal than a subordinate.

Start the conversation. I attended a private dinner for *Inc.* magazine's Women's Summit and had the honor of sitting next to Kevin O'Leary, of the hit show *Shark Tank.* I do not drink often and was unaware that Kevin O'Leary was in the wine business. However, I didn't want this moment to pass without starting a conversation, so I said, "Kevin, I see you have a few bottles of white wine here. Can you recommend one for someone who doesn't drink but prefers a floral aftertaste?" That sparked his interest immediately, and he went into a long discussion about wine. Before I knew it, I was tasting Pinot Grigio, Chardonnay, and Chablis. I wasn't interested in the wine—I was interested in the conversation because this could make a great mentorship opportunity.

From the weather to events on the news—except for politics—start the conversation. Shifting perception is about taking the initiative to engage. Although wine is not a typical topic for me, it was a common, convenient, and relevant one at that particular dinner. I'm sure Kevin O'Leary has had a million people walk up to him and talk about *Shark Tank,* but fewer people ask about his wine business. I didn't want to talk about the show, I wanted to exchange ideas if possible. Find a common focal point, and start the conversation. Don't wait to be invited, as highly effective leaders always make the first move. The following gives an example of how to start:

Ice Breaker

Good Morning, _____

I just heard that we are expecting another foot of snow tomorrow.

Can you believe this weather?

When I leave today, I am going to stock up on groceries just in case.

Do you have any plans?

This is a light and neutral conversation starter that can open up a dialogue. Avoid personal issues, such as politics or religion—it may work against you. Start with weather or local events, but find something and use it as a conversation starter. Also, when decision makers observe you starting a conversation with a gatekeeper, there is a likelihood that they would like to know who you are, because you are engaging with another leader. The level of accessibility sparks curiosity, and those are the conversations that are being held about you outside of your presence.

Three Ways to Leave Your Mark in the Office Without Saying a Word

Effective communication has several layers, which are deeply rooted in trust. When you're communicating, it is imperative to build trust and credibility before commencing a conversation. If decision makers, gatekeepers, stakeholders, or colleagues believe they can trust you, they are receptive to your advice and opinions. You have to set the perception and leave your mark on people who are connected to your professional ascension.

Here are three ways to achieve their trust and leave your mark.

1. Control Your Posture

Decision makers are watching, and every interaction or conversation is a visual experience. Ever since a chance meeting with a *Forbes* contributor at Starbucks, I take simple trips, like ones to the supermarket, seriously because I never know the encounters I could have at Trader Joe's. "Ninety-three percent of communication occurs through nonverbal behavior and tone; only 7 percent of communication takes place through the use of words," says John Stoker, the author of *Overcoming Fake Talk: How to Hold Real Conversations That Create Respect, Build Relationships, and Get Results.* Although we all know the adage "be yourself," or "we shouldn't care what other people think," the business of leadership is not as forgiving, especially for women. Our body language beginning with how we carry ourselves speaks volumes about who we are and who we think we are. Here are some elements of body language to be aware of:

- Shoulders back
- Head high
- Legs together
- Put on your best power outfit
- Capture their attention

Before we get to how to communicate effectively, we have to get you in the posture to communicate. To build a rapport with any gatekeeper or decision maker, you have to let them see you in action. No more shrugging shoulders and sitting down to speak. Elevate your voice and get into your high-power posture. High-power leaders are not sitting and competing for their voices to be heard. They are standing up, commanding all attention, and shining a spotlight on themselves so the team knows who the leader is. Even if your voice is trembling, stand up. Even if you don't think you have the answer, stand up. Even if you are afraid of rejection, stand up.

2. Pose

When I was invited to give my first TED Talk, it was an honor of my lifetime. Standing on that famous red circle carpet was an emotional moment. I wasn't aware of all of the preparation and choreography leading up to a TED Talk, but it is heavily rooted in posture and posing. The ability to stand erect for eight minutes, while remembering all of your takeaways and transition points, is an amazing skill in itself. With my speeches in the past, I sometimes had notes near the timer to guide me, but this talk required my full memorization with no sudden moves. I had to command the room while making a power pose.

Clear communication will require you to get out of your comfort zone. You may think that you have been effective in meetings by speaking up and contributing value while sitting down. Maybe decision makers have been listening to you, but have they seen you? Let me share my top three power poses for women leaders:

Put your hands on your hips. This is my favorite stance when speaking to any decision maker in a casual capacity, by the water cooler or in the lobby for example. It allows you to exude confidence without the need to hunch your back over or minimize your significance in their presence.

Place your hands on the table and lean forward. This is the best pose for meetings. Leaning forward while standing shows dominance. I recommend this pose in meetings and events.

Lift your arms high and celebrate. This is a great pose when you are congratulating your team or celebrating a major victory.

3. Make a Great First Impression

We all have that one outfit that makes us feel invincible. I have a maroon A-line dress that changes my mood and increases my confidence. Communication starts with a visual cue before moving to a conversation. In my experience with Debbie's initial in-person presentation, I worried about the potential backlash from my audience, considering it was also my first impression to an audience of thousands.

I am not suggesting a full makeover, but think about self-perception for a moment:

- What does your appearance say about you?
- Do you look like the leader you want to be?

- What do you think decision makers are saying about you in closed rooms?
- Do you believe your promotion has been compromised due to your appearance?
- Who is the leader you most admire? Describe this person's appearance. How can you achieve a similar look?
- What are some simple fixes you can implement?

"We all want to be judged on our merits and not a workplace dress code. However, the way you present yourself *does* affect your professional capacity. It affects how others perceive you. It affects your reputation. Ultimately, it affects your ability to be productive and get things done," states a blog by Time Management Ninjas called *How Your Professional Appearance Affects Your Productivity.*

If you want to have your name plate on the door of the C-suite, you need to earn trust, and doing so can happen upon first impressions and formed perceptions. Trust leads to decision makers asking for your opinion, listening to you when you talk, and raving about you behind closed doors. In other words, a positive perception is what gains you respect, and when you are respected a cycle of professionalism is ensured. Once you create the perception in the office, then you can distance yourself from the "nice girl" image and eliminate the stereotypes that keep women away from the C-suite, and doors will open.

3

What's Like Got to Do with It?

The Rewards of Respect

KEY TAKEAWAY

Likability in life and your career is not the goal. Respect is the goal—earning it, keeping it, exuding it, and building on it.

I have a cousin who was one of the cool kids in the neighborhood. Growing up a child of immigrants, I marveled at how my cousin so easily adopted American culture. She donned trendy door-knocker hoop earrings, a cool asymmetrical haircut, the most modern clothes, but most importantly, she could jump rope Double Dutch style. I was not well-versed in the secular life or pop culture of the day; my pigtailed eight-year-old self knew more about the *Wall Street Journal* and the *New York Times* than MC Lyte. My cousin and her friends were at a local block party engaging in a Double Dutch competition—jumping Brooklyn style, with old-fashioned wire phone cords for the jump rope, under the streetlamp with a small boom box, while blasting Rob Base's hit song, *It takes two*, at the highest decibel level possible—I was left out, a spectator on the sidelines, a nonparticipant in the rhythm and cadence of skipping chants and rhymes.

As the girls jumped rope, I had no idea what songs they were singing, or why "Miss Penny called the lady with the alligator purse." Yet, I imitated them, mouthing words to make it look like I knew the songs. I begged my cousin to let me jump rope with her, but to no avail. She must have known that most certainly I would trip on my first try, and in doing so embarrass her in front of her cool friends. Finally, after enough nagging, she gave in.

Her friends turned the rope, and my cousin told me to follow the count—5, 4, 3, 2, 1—before I jumped in. Well, upon entry, the rope caught my ankle, and instantly I lost the game for the whole team. *What a loser*, I thought. I was nothing more than a fraud trying to fit into a group that would never accept me because I was different. I was a nerd. I could hear the bevy of voices snickering, "I don't like her." If only I could find a way for them to "like" me, my cousin would accept me. For that to happen, I'd need to change my interests. Stop reading the real estate sections on Sundays. I'd need to part with my braids and go for the shave. Then I'd be invited to skip Double Dutch.

The psychology of attraction reveals many reasons people like us and why we like certain people in return. Among them are relatability and common interests, being physically appealing, and proximity. Attempting to force people to like you or accept you—whether it be through imitation, acquiescence, or plain old tagging along—will cause you to have to uphold an act or performance that will never be sustainable. The role-playing, aside from being utterly exhausting, will ultimately trip up your ankle with a jump rope of your own making. For far too many women, no matter how far they've gotten in life or how much they've achieved in their career trajectory, continue to compete in an imaginary Double Dutch competition.

You don't know how to skip one rope, not to mention two! And whether you can or not won't guarantee people will like you. In fact, the first step into the no explanation lifestyle is normalizing the fact that, especially in your professional journey, not all people will like you.

Some people may not gel with your personality, may not share the same values, or may alienate you out of envy. Likability in life and your career is not the goal. Respect is the goal: earning it, keeping it, exuding it, building on it. But how can we focus on such serious matters when being a woman in the workplace can feel like checking the weather before going outside, taking the temperatures of our environment and the various people within it:

- Is this the day to smile?
- Is this the day to be upset?
- Am I smiling enough?
- Do I look approachable?
- Do I look upset?

We get so many mixed messages on what it takes to be respected in the workplace, we tend to default back on the likability characteristics, never recognizing the actions that signal and secure our respect.

I spent so much of my life trying to find ways to be accepted and "liked." I realize now that when I entered corporate America, I tried to build friendships and relationships. I thought the goal was to work during the day and have happy hour in the evening with my coworkers. For a few years, I crossed the line several times, inviting coworkers to my home and sharing experiences in my personal life, which left me vulnerable to judgments and attacks. I misinterpreted the meaning of the workplace. I thought that if I focused on my likability factor, these people would help me get to the top. Subsequently, all of those "friendships" worked against me. I was passed up for every opportunity for professional growth because instead of building relationships with key decision makers and gatekeepers, I was focused on having parties and gatherings with people who could never help me to grow in my career. I was also not surrounded by like-minded people, wasting my time being popular with people who did not have my level of ambition. The perception of the decision makers was that I was only as good as the crowd I hung out with, and about as serious: guilty by association.

While I was laughing and trying to be accepted, some of the same colleagues I had confided in were being taken seriously because they knew how to play the game. I was naive and thought that just showing up for work every day, putting on a great outfit, working overtime, and smiling every morning was more than enough to get noticed. I didn't prove myself to be worthy of a promotion or an advancement; I just proved that I was the office confidant. As I continued to be alienated by some of my colleagues, who were quickly moving up the ladder into the C-suite, I had to redirect some of my energy and focus onto how to change my mindset to grasp the fact that I was losing a significant amount of my equity at work. In my quest to be liked, I was forgoing the only road that mattered: the one that leads to respect.

I partly blame myself for not understanding the significance of earning respect at work. After my internship with the Brooklyn DA, I worked with a woman named Deborah at a boutique law firm in Garden City, New York, and I always saw her as playful, nice, thoughtful, and more as a friend than an attorney. Deborah used to hang out with many of the interns and support staff at a local restaurant after work, and I enjoyed her company. She kept all of us laughing, but Deborah had a completely different personality—an alter ego—in the presence of the partners. At work, amongst the partners, who were all male, she was the only woman who had an invitation into some of the partnership-level meetings. I viewed her humbleness and humor as more of a friend than a colleague, but when the announcement was made that she had made partner, I realized she knew how to earn respect. She had one personality for the support staff and another for all of the partners. The announcement blindsided me because other women who worked at the firm seemed to be disturbed by her success. Today, Deborah has moved on from being a partner in a boutique law firm to the owner and head partner of her own commercial litigation law firm on Wall Street, with a roster of noteworthy clients such as Target and Walgreens. We stay in touch on social media; her jokes on her Instagram live posts have me in stitches, but I am well aware that she has boundaries, which led her from being a law student to an associate to a partner to an owner—and one of her male associates happens to be one of the founding partners of the firm we used to work for.

Deborah took the road leading to respect first and also was a likable person. She did not allow likability to overshadow her ascension into the C-suite. She commanded respect and was invited into high-level rooms where decisions were being made, and although I had not seen her in action, she had certainly added value. Only a select few women I have ever worked with in law firms have ever made it to the partnership level, and it continues to be rare due to disparities in pay and investment levels (you have to pay to have your name on the door of the top law firms, sometimes in the high six figures). She has always been to me a leading example of how to be liked *and* respected.

A Fine Line

There is a difference between being liked and being respected, and women are often unfairly forced to choose between the two. On one hand, being liked will give you social capital in the office, because you are kind, approachable, polite, and agreeable. I define gaining respect at work as setting boundaries and articulating clear intentions as a leader. Some women are conditioned to believe this is rigid and aggressive, but neither quality need apply. Respect does not require you to be mean or assertive, but it does require clarity, which is the opposite of how you will be viewed in the office when you're liked. Common phrases such as "I have an open-door policy" or "let me know if you ever need anything" will be hard to uphold when you focus on respect. You can have an open-door policy, but you must discern who you grant access to such a policy. When you focus on respect, you cannot be everything to everyone. Caroline Fairchild, Editor at Large at LinkedIn, stated in a LinkedIn article titled, "For Women, Being "Liked" at Work Is a Double-Edged Sword," women leaders are four times more likely than men to be seen as collaborative in the workplace. It goes on to state that, "We also need to place more women— women with all sorts of personalities, leadership styles and mannerisms—into positions of power. Only then will the pressure lessen for female leaders to be both 'likeable' and 'perfect' at work."

Erin Loos Cutraro, chief executive and founder of She Should Run, stated in "The Likability Trap Is Still a Thing," an article published in the *New York Times,* "We expect women to be both highly qualified *and* likable," while "men are seen as strong and electable simply because they're men." This is a setup for failure, because if we feel we must be liked, we overcommunicate and justify our decisions using passive language and details that make us vulnerable and open to being coerced and manipulated. Our demeanor changes, which affects the outcome of how we articulate ourselves. If you believe you are in front of people you like and who like you, chances are you're going to be more friendly, less direct, and a bit vague, especially if you've had them over to your house for happy hour. We will talk about how to defend against this trap of passiveness in Chapters 8 and 9.

I can honestly say I gave away tens of thousands of dollars in the course of business because I did not have nonnegotiable boundaries nor did I command respect in the beginning. I don't want you to fall into the same traps I did.

My Lesson with Likability

When I first started my transition into the real estate investing game, one of my first transactions was a rehab project on two acres of prime real estate in North Carolina. With very little money and no relationships, I needed a partner to help me fund the deal. I was introduced to a couple, who also happened to be pastors in a local church, who were very interested in the property. They were warm and welcoming, and we instantly connected. They invited me to their home and I met their children. I was impressed by all of their accolades within the real estate community. Within a matter of weeks, we went to tour the property and they promised to help me fund the deal for a percentage of the profit.

I found a basic operating agreement on Google and they signed it, but I did not know that there were so many parameters within the agreement that would not fully protect my interests if I were circumvented. Why would I think of anything like that since I thought they were trustworthy? A few weeks went by, and all of our communication became scarce. It just happened that one day, I was in the area of the property, and I noticed a heavy amount of construction taking place. This was odd because we had not closed on the purchase of the property. I called the seller to find out if he had changed his mind about the sale, to which he replied, "No, we went to closing a few days ago." The seller also went on to say, "I want to thank you so much for introducing me to the pastors because now that the property is sold, I can move on to other projects." I had no idea that these pastors had worked out a deal without me and closed on the property in a secret transaction. Enraged, I called them to collect my share of the profits.

"I don't know what you're talking about," the pastor said. "We don't owe you anything; you made an introduction and we closed. End of story."

We'll talk later about rash reactions versus thoughtful responses, but let's just say I reacted . . . passionately. We exchanged some heated words, most of which I am ashamed to repeat, but I was angry. The next morning, I filed a small claims suit against them. When we arrived at court, the pastors entered the courthouse masterfully dressed in their clergy cloaks, indicating a well-rehearsed serial scam. Both pastors told the judge they didn't remember signing an agreement with me; they had thought that I wanted their autograph to sell on eBay. This spectacle of lies went on for two hours; the judge ruled in their favor. As we walked out of the courtroom, they unzipped the robes, looked at me, and laughed. The joke was on me: the pastors went on to make about half a million dollars in profit on that one home, of which I never saw a dime.

That was my first and last trip to the court, and probably one of the best lessons I ever learned. Focusing on being liked caused me to blindly trust people who did not have my best interest in mind. When you reveal too much, people spot your weaknesses and make a play for them. The pastors sensed I had set up an expectation of validation instead of value. In her TED Talk, "The Likability Dilemma," Robin Hauser said, "Women who negotiate for themselves are perceived as selfish and women who negotiate on behalf of someone else are perceived to be helpful, and a helpful woman might be liked more . . . but the helpful woman will not be recognized as having what it takes to be a successful leader." This was a valuable lesson on the importance of setting the ground rules for respect and outcomes.

The Psychology of Likable

Why do people like certain people and not others? What compels someone to conform to someone else's standards in an attempt to win approval? It may be harmful in your career, as you may have to adhere to a level that could be below your value. Women often get caught in a trap of middle management historically because they're unsure of what to expect from the next level, which commonly has had a horrible reputation. If you've ever watched the movie *The Devil Wears Prada*, you may understand this theory, where it appears that a woman in leadership has to be shrewd, with an unapproachable demeanor to be a leader. All of these are myths, but once you open up and see yourself being liked, it is difficult to earn the respect of decision makers and gate-keepers in the C-suite.

You can be both liked and respected at work, as long as you set the framework that will guide your interactions, which I will demonstrate later in this chapter. But on the seesaw of personality traits that are effective in accelerating your path to leadership, it is more productive to be respected than to be liked. "High-achieving women experience social backlash because their very success—and specifically the behaviors that created that success—violates our expectations about how women are supposed to behave. Women are expected to be nice, warm, friendly, and nurturing," according to an article by Marianne Cooper in the *Harvard Business Review*, titled "For Women Leaders, Likability and Success Hardly Go Hand-in-Hand."

There are a few distinct differences between liking people and respecting them. I recently sent out a request for contractors for a roofing project on a local website. On the day of the open call, 20 contractors came to the job site and claimed that they were ready to do the roofing job based on the request for a quote that was listed. One by one, they all measured, and I must say they were all friendly and nice, but there were only two in the entire group that showed up on that cold morning that I respected. Everyone was likable, but only two were prepared with an estimate and evidence to substantiate the investment. By setting the groundwork early in our conversation, they were able to build trust and a rapport with my team. They were prepared to prove themselves to win over not just one job, but all of the collective roofing jobs we could potentially have in the future. The personalities are all the same, but very few provide the framework to substantiate their qualifications. For that, I deeply respected both contractors, and I have worked with both of them on subsequent jobs as well.

The Flip-Flop Philosophy

Women are magnets for mixed messages. One day, they say wear suits, the next day they say wear pants, smile, red lipstick, blue lipstick, high heels, stilettos, jeans—it's a miracle that some of us want to continue this journey at all. When it comes to gaining respect and the qualities one needs to exude to earn it, the rules of the game are constantly changing—but only for women. Sometimes you don't even know if you should smile at work, or if you should come into work wearing your emotions on your sleeve. The other day, I read a report that said it's okay to cry at work. The next morning there was a segment on the local news that said women have to hold back their tears if they want to get ahead. There are so many mixed messages that it is hard to know how to be respected, so this is another goalpost-moving piece of advice, but it has worked for hundreds of women that I have worked with within my company. Find a balance between advancing in your career and socializing.

Three Boundaries That Build Respect

Maintain a Standard for How You Are Addressed

At an important business meeting in San Francisco that had taken three months to secure, I found myself the only woman among 14 men in the room. To my dismay and against my wishes, word had gotten out that my father had lost his cancer battle just two days prior. "Babe, I'm so sorry for your loss," one attendee said, which led to the other man saying, "Honey, sorry you're going through this right now." And the next man chimed in, "Sweetie, you're in my prayers." I had to shift the focus onto the agenda.

I replied, "To be clear, my name is not babe, honey, or sweetie. My name is Carol. I thank you for all of your well wishes during this difficult time and appreciate your concern. But if we can agree to call each other by our first names, and only our first names, I think it is most appropriate."

Allowing terms of endearment shifts the priority from respect to like, and that was not the purpose of making a cross-country trip, versus postponing or canceling the meeting during such a solemn time in my life. I have boundaries and standards, and I had to set the clear expectation that the babe, honey, gumdrop thing doesn't work with me. I maintain the same standard with women who call me "sis" or "sweetheart." Unless we have that relationship, I don't do it to anyone, and I don't expect it to be done to me. When we conflate lines of respect, unintentionally we settle for less than we deserve—and that's why some meetings in the C-suite never happen for women. If a decision maker calls you "sweetie" during the meeting and you don't clarify your position, it indicates that you are not clearly communicating your boundaries and expectations.

I have the same standard for my tenants. Some are a little bit older, and when it's time to do property inspections, they love to call me "sweetheart," seeing me as their granddaughter and not their landlord. I always have to shift the focus back, saying, "If I call you Mr. Jackson, you can call me Mrs. Sankar. If I call you Bob, you can call me Carol. There's no need to cross any lines because I deserve the same respect that I give you. I have a standard of how I want to be treated and a standard of how I believe you need to be treated, and as long as we stay along that line, we can achieve great things."

As women, we have a way of lightheartedly accepting terms of endearment in professional settings and justifying it as a joke or vernacular. We rarely witness men having the same interactions at work or senior-level women interacting in the same manner. When was the last time you heard the VP of sales call the CFO "Bro" or "Buddy" during a strategy meeting? Women normalize lower-level standards, beginning with de-individualizing themselves using fluffy nicknames, and then wonder why we cannot get ahead. The moment your manager—man or woman—starts calling you "honey," neither has any intention of giving you access to the C-suite. They have demoted your access without you ever having the chance to first express your intent. When you focus on being respected, you start with how people address you, and you work your way down to create the level of attention and expectation for people to treat you.

Prioritize the Day

The number one priority at work is productivity. Although it is important to build relationships, it is equally important to prioritize every moment of the day to ensure that every task has a measurable value—such as making 10 introductory or sales calls by the end of the day or measuring the success of your social media ad campaigns and analyzing the data. From the meetings you attend to the emails you respond to, and even some of the after-work social networks—it is important to have a list of priorities each day. Decision makers and gatekeepers pay close attention to your effectiveness daily. That's how they determine promotions and leadership roles; if you can be the most effective member of the team, you will possibly be on their watch list. Rather than spending the morning gossiping at the water cooler or standing at a colleague's desk talking about something you watched on Netflix, stick to your tasks at hand so that you can gain a high level of respect at work.

To achieve this, you must create a list of deliverables, expectations, and intentions for the day. Here are some great ways to prioritize your day:

- **Make a list.** Make a list of the most important tasks of the day at least 24 hours in advance, and create a road map to achieve a result by the end of the day.
- **Prioritize your emails.** Create a folder in your inbox of priority emails that must be addressed first thing in the morning when you enter the office. That level of engagement in the first part of the day allows you to have more time to effectively solve problems for the rest of the day. Rather than respond to a difficult customer or client in the afternoon, which could interrupt your productivity, make it your top priority in the morning.
- **Create relationships over lunch.** I consistently reference relationships throughout this book, and the best time to create relationships is over lunch. There's

nothing better than a lunch meeting to have short and guided conversations and interactions with decision makers. Instead of using lunchtime as relaxation time, use that time to get into the direct eyesight of all of the gatekeepers who need to know your name. It doesn't have to be formal, but you will gain their respect if you find a way to get on their calendar. A lunch meeting is one of the most important meetings you'll ever have in your career—don't waste it sitting in a lunchroom with your colleagues and gossiping. Spend that time advancing your career as a leader.

- **Be approachable, yet work in silence.** If you manage to be invited to lunch with a gatekeeper or decision maker, express your professional ambitions, but keep their advice guarded. Those conversations are confidential, but they are mentorship meetings. The higher you go in your career, the more you will have to make high-level moves in silence. If you want to gain the respect of decision makers, they have to know that you are willing to keep the conversations you engage in during your lunch meetings confidential.

- **Take the lead.** Whenever possible, if there is a work-related project or an assignment that could use a leader in any capacity, don't look around the room—raise your head and take the lead. You earn the respect of your colleagues by moving forward and taking on challenging assignments, not lowering your head and hoping not to be called on. Don't wait for anyone to find you: raise your hand and be seen. Whether you are qualified or not, the first act of courage to gain respect is taking the lead. There have been many times when I have taken on projects where I had no idea where to start, but somehow, the level of responsibility helped me to become a problem solver. It also allowed me to gain the respect of other decision makers. It is also a great way for you to build relationships with mentors and advisors who will help you succeed.

Reclaim Your Time

Part of my sternness around time is to ensure that every minute of an encounter is used productively. For example, if we have an introductory call at noon just to get acquainted and identify any professional synergy, I expect that you are on the call before noon, because only the minutes after 12 are the ones that I will count as productive. If we land on the call before noon, let's say 11:55 a.m., then we can exchange a few moments of small talk. I must stick to an agenda that leads to a favorable result, and that cannot be done unless I set the intention early for our meeting. I have the same expectation of almost every element of my professional life. If we are supposed to meet at a specific time, if you want to have a glass of wine before the meeting, I'm up for it. But at the time the meeting begins, everything is business from then until the end of the scheduled time. The goal is to ensure that people respect my values. Besides, I don't give my time easily.

Getting on my calendar is quite difficult, and there are layers of people who discern the importance of every meeting before it even gets to my calendar. There are only a few situations where I'm personally involved, but I have a long list of calls, meetings, and emails that I will not respond to, simply because I try to ensure that we save our time within the company for stakeholders, decision makers, and clients, rather than having unguided conversations without a direct result.

None of this means, however, that I don't laugh and joke with my team or decision makers. Completely the opposite: I sprinkle a lot of humor into my respect routine. I am funny and gracious, but I set my intentions early in every meeting by starting with, "What I hope we can accomplish within the next 20 minutes together is an accurate budget to meet next month's sales target." I make sure that I outline my expectations, and I'm very meticulous about my time. If I say that I only have four minutes, believe me, I'm leaving in four minutes.

When people understand your boundaries, they understand that there's a time to laugh and a time to do business. It also works well when decision makers can see that you have specific standards and know-how to balance your priorities, which will be no different in the C-suite. When you learn how to command respect, you're less likely to apologize when communicating, because it's an expectation that you have specific standards.

If all along you focus on being liked, the day that you decide to set a standard or a boundary, you will be compelled to apologize publicly and over explain the sudden change when it is time to enforce it. No one needs to fear you to respect you, you just have to set nonnegotiable boundaries very early and people will still like you.

How To Create Your Respect Routine

Make Yourself an Asset

There comes a moment in your career when you need to recognize the difference between an asset and a liability. Assets focus on performance and ascending further in their career. They are irreplaceable to the success of their team and company and are viewed as revenue generators. When a gate-keeper presents a selected pool of vested in-house talent for promotion, it normally starts with revenue: "Janet is our lead sales director for the acquisitions department, who helped us close $10 million last quarter. I think she should be considered for the role of VP of this department." On the other hand, a liability is stationary at a comfortable position and rarely takes any risks. I have a few friends who proudly proclaim themselves to be a liability at work because they are afraid of the responsibility that comes with management roles. It is not negative at all, but they are not interested in career growth.

Although these are terms related to finance, they're very helpful to explain the process of navigating toward the C-suite. Once you become an asset, the quality of your work and relationships become intentional: meaning everything you do, everyone you meet, every goal you set has an identi-fied purpose—an intention to accelerate your career. This is the stage where the value of introductions matters. It is also the stage where what people say about you when you're not in the room will change your career path.

Gatekeepers to every decision maker are watching you in silence and making decisions about promotions and rec-ommendations outside of the typical workday. Focusing on creating a level of respect will yield positive results, which makes it easier for you to communicate your value and gain influence to climb the leadership ladder.

Set Expectations

Every interaction in your career must end with a deliverable. For example, as I mentioned earlier about the importance of requesting lunch meetings, when you send the request, make sure you include a reason for the invitation and a few topics you would like to cover during your limited time together. A vague request may not attract a response, but when you are specific, especially if you include an agenda, it will attract attention. Limit all conversations or correspondence that do not yield results. It's a matter of prioritizing your time effectively by setting a productivity schedule.

For example, let's say someone asked to get on the phone with you and pick your brain about your expertise, an appropriate response could be (choose one or all):

- Can you provide a list of three questions in advance to guide our discussion?
- Please provide a full agenda and the outcomes you hope to gain from this conversation within the next 24 hours so my team can decide how to proceed.
- Is it possible to have this conversation via email?
- You're welcome to send a request through to my administrative department, and they will let you know of my availability.

You must choose a response that is strategic and direct. Most of all, your response must indicate that you understand the value of your time. A common phobia that professional women struggle with is simply saying no. It may sound a bit rigid, but it will help you increase productivity by discerning the importance of the request before responding. In addition, it will help you to create effective and timely responses in advance to avoid reacting to inquiries, which we will discuss soon.

Stay In Your Lane

The lesson I learned from trying to jump Double Dutch with my cousin and her friends was that I always knew it was not for me. I've tried that same trick many times, and always ended up with the same result—failure. When you stay in your lane, avoiding the need to fit in with others at work, decision makers notice. This doesn't mean you should alienate yourself from other colleagues, coworkers, and associates, it simply means you are aware of your strengths and there is no need to talk yourself into playing Double Dutch when you are only great at hopscotch. Even if you play alone, someone will notice and either join you or ask you to teach them how to play the game.

I have met many women who try too hard at work to be an imitation of everyone else while limiting themselves. The impact of trying to "fit in" has a direct effect on why women focus on likability. Besides, it is easy to follow the crowd, and I understand that need. But your unique skills will open specific doors that are related to your specialty. You were onboarded because you offer something unique. Don't fall into the trap of doing what everyone else does just to be accepted. It is an easy trap to fall into, and one of the reasons why the glass cliff—women who have been offered short-term seats in the C-suite to fill quotas—is disproportionately impacting women. Remember to bring your authentic self and your specific expertise to your career. It is a door opener and a game changer.

4

Activating Your Alter Ego
A Super Power for Performance

KEY TAKEAWAY

The highest performing businesspeople, celebrities, and athletes adopt a mindset that enables them to separate from insecurities, fear, and indecisiveness.

I am fearless in front of the stage, but a few days before an appearance, I am an emotional wreck. Lifelong programmed insecurities, limiting self-talk, and the traditional role I was taught to play in life—a quiet, pleasing girl—attempt their invasion into my mind. I have strategies, no doubt, to combat these forces: breathing, positive messages, and saying out loud into the mirror, like a good friend would, "Shake it off, Carol. You've got this!"

Every single time I walk onstage beneath the lights, in front of an audience of ambitious and intelligent people, a wave of calm and confidence pulls me into a zone. Later, in my dressing room, replaying and critiquing my performance, I berate myself, "What made you so worked up, Carol?" I say, as I stand in front of the mirror removing layers of makeup. "You always worry for no reason. Stop doubting yourself!"

And so goes the roller coaster of doubt and confidence—the climbs and dips of anxiety and exhilaration that make my stomach drop. It took a few years to figure out why I do this to myself: one minute, an emotional basket case with complete amnesia for how many times I've nailed an appearance, and the next minute, an activated, capable version of myself conquering the world.

As most things do, my insecurities date back to my upbringing as a young first-generation American, with a Caribbean accent that made me stand out in the classroom. Although I was raised in the United States, I grew up in a home speaking Patois, a common dialect with heavy French, British, Dutch, and Portuguese influences mixed with English. There were moments when I mixed up some common English words, such as *mushrooms* and *onion* (in Patois, *jumbery* and *cive*, respectively).

By the time I was a teenager, the thought of speaking in front of the class at school, or partaking in any task that involved speaking in public, caused a debilitating panic. The thought of the class laughing if I answered a question wrong, or mocking my Caribbean accent, prompted me to talk my way out of presenting. "People with social anxiety believe that social situations pose a danger," according to David M. Clark and Adrian Wells's cognitive behavioral model of social phobia as referenced in PsychologyTools.com. "They fear negative evaluation, believing in particular that they are in danger of behaving in an inept and unacceptable fashion, and that such behavior will have disastrous consequences in terms of loss of status, loss of worth, and rejection."

In my former days in corporate America, it was clear that there was no way around public speaking, especially in the law firm world. Except, as Clark and Wells described, I was fighting against the danger of being "found out" and exposed as a lesser-than performer who would act differently and "disastrously" and sabotage my road to the C-suite. I was focused on refraining from mixing Patois and English at work to avoid the "Where are you from?" question, which made my anxiety tailspin.

The problem with being this purposeful about my speech was that at my early level there wasn't an opportunity for scripted, carefully planned presentations that wowed the right people. The way to get noticed on the lower ladder rungs was to orate my ideas in an impromptu setting—with no scripts, no preparation, just speaking and adding the most value when I found the chance.

So I had a choice to make: stay scripted and silent or find a way to protect myself from my fear. I needed to create a layer—a shield—to guard myself against overthinking, or else these insecurities would pummel my career and my sanity. That's when I discovered the alter ego, which some psychologists and researchers refer to as self-distancing. According to an article by David Robson published by BBC, titled "The Batman Effect: How Having an Alter Ego Empowers You," self-distancing is when you create space from your feelings in the moment so you can allow yourself to view a situation less emotionally. "Self-distancing seems to enable people to reap these positive effects by leading them to focus on the bigger picture—it's possible to see events as part of a broader plan rather than getting bogged down in immediate feelings," says Robson.

Think of Yourself in the Third Person

We all have memories of performing in front of the mirror, pretending to be a superstar, invisible mic in hand, dance moves that would make Janet Jackson jealous. We didn't know when we were 11 that we were trying on our alter ego: confident and badass after a day of being invisible in the schoolyard or picked last for manhunt. The alter ego you projected in the mirror is the same alter ego you need to bring to your career if you want to smash the glass and walk into the C-suite. It's cloaking yourself in a layer of confidence to bring with you every day as you take your journey toward leadership.

This book is centered on combating passive communication that sabotages the C-suite sensibility. But really the first stop before utilizing language and fighting against passive reactions and phrases is to create and exude a mindset, body language, an alternative personality—and even wardrobe—that act as vessels and catalysts for powerful language. You won't tell someone no firmly (and without explanation) if your head is held low and you are silently calling yourself a loser, or if you aren't mirroring your industry's image.

Enter your alter ego. She stands upright, she knows she is capable and valuable and talented, and she is ready to firmly and respectfully prove her doubters wrong. (And if you want to give her a cape, go ahead and do that, too!) According to a *Forbes* article, "Step Up to 2020 with an Alter Ego," the third-person treatment provides separateness that reduces threat. "These personas allow people to take risks, then depersonalize encounters."

When we adopt an alter ego, it changes our posture, allows us to make more eye contact, and even helps us become more animated in our presentation style in public settings. Honestly, it is a game changer, and many high-power leaders are aware of the impact of posture and positioning and its effect on commanding attention as a leader.

I've hosted numerous events with high-level women who struggle with some of the same issues I have—and then some. This is especially true if you are a woman of color, an older woman, or an immigrant woman. The constant need to reassure yourself that you belong in the room is a feeling that doesn't go away on its own. One way to overcome some of your own self-biases is to create and build an alter ego that allows you to be the kind of leader you want to be while guarding your insecurities. I think we can agree that we are all working to improve ourselves while in a constant battle to unlearn specific behaviors from our past. We all have some level of trauma, and it takes time to work through it, but the C-suite is not going to wait for you to get it together. The journey requires you to articulate clearly and have a level of confidence—and for many women, for the reasons just stated, this is only possible when they induce an out-of-body experience.

When I adopted the alter ego, my goal was (and still is) to influence decision makers to focus on what I offer instead of "what I am." The further up you move on the leadership ladder, the questions become tougher, the conversations more engaged, and the network has higher stakes. The same personality that helped you land your first job when you were 18 will not be the same one needed in your thirties, forties, or beyond. Your level of expression must change, and it requires you to articulate your value *on the spot*. That leaves little room and time for doubt and inferiority complexes. Real leaders are problem solvers, and you never know the level of difficulty or importance of your next problem. You will be tested, and some situations will require you to be under a microscope. Criticisms will feel like attacks; some of them will be. They are not personal, but designed to test if you know how to solve big problems—and whether you remain unwavering under the knowledge of who you are.

Although I talk, teach, research, and write about confidence in women leaders, some self-sabotaging habits are almost impossible to break. The habit of worry and the consistent replay of negative scenarios in your mind is difficult to unlearn, especially if you couple it with the story that you tell yourself. I call this habit the "that will never happen for me" mindset, where you invest in the belief that the journey to the C-suite is one of luck, rather than skill and communication. Whether you're blaming your race, gender, sexuality, or socioeconomic demographic—there's always some level of learned behavior that prevents you from entering rooms and taking risks. Besides, women are naturally risk averse, and it is a primary reason why we tend to lean toward women-centric professions (which I will talk about in the next chapter), instead of taking risks in male-dominated industries or high-growth businesses.

If you have a difficult time breaking free of the habit of worry, it will be impossible for you to gain the courage to go to the C-suite if you don't adopt some level of superficial protection to guard yourself against potential harm, especially if you are a sensitive person. Most of us do not like to admit it, we publicize our fears, as we have not found a way to separate the person from the persona that will yield positive results in the C-suite. The rest of this chapter acts as your proverbial phone booth, in which you will learn to transform yourself from woman to superwoman.

Living the Double Life

Kobe Bryant had Black Mamba and Dwayne Johnson has The Rock. LeBron James, Michael Jordan, Sia, Adele, and Pink all have alter egos. Beyoncé calls hers Sasha Fierce, and believe me, if you have ever been to a live performance, you can see the intensity that Sasha Fierce brings to the show. At the end of the show, Sasha Fierce waves goodbye and Beyoncé humbly appears for a moment and cries.

What's your alter ego? For the regular everyday person, I describe an alter ego as playing a role, adopting a persona, slipping into character, or simply changing your mindset in the moment. For some women, every time they see an opportunity they think they are suited for, a level of debilitating insecurity shows up to talk them out of it. Having an alter ego will place you in the type of rooms you've only dreamed of.

Creating an alter ego allows you to separate yourself personally from any level of judgment or fear. Imagine having the courage to say what you need to say at the moment it needs to be said, and with clarity. That is something that might be the job for your alter ego. I have also heard some celebrities refer to this concept as their manufactured identity. Their level of greatness can only be displayed when they do not feel the direct impact of criticism and judgment, and they are rewarded for their level of confidence. There are many ways to tap into your confident persona: from theme music to meditation to striking a pose—whichever way works for you, find a way to get in your zone. I access my alter ego by listening to motivational clips on YouTube before each appearance. It helps me clear out the noise in my mind and focus on the goal ahead.

In 2015, I gave a talk at an event in Rochester, New York, before an audience of about 7,000 people. The room was dark, as the entire event was recorded for future use in one of the sponsor's courses; the speakers could only hear the audience, not see them. On the morning of the event, the event coordinator came into the greenroom to share that they were having technical difficulties with their green screens that had our presentation slides uploaded. I was not worried at all. However, the speaker ahead of me had a panic attack. She kept going back and forth to the sound engineer, asking, "How long until you find out when the green screen will be back? I can't do this talk without slides." All I could hear from my dressing room was, "We're working on it ma'am, we're working on it." The moment the glitch was fixed, she was relieved. My alter ego had already arrived, and she made the difference between me slipping into self-sabotaging fear and remaining poised and ready to go.

When the announcer called the first speaker's name, she went to the stage with her clicker in hand and began her speech. I watched from the greenroom, but things quickly turned the moment she made the first click. The green screen was not working again. In front of 7,000 people, she had a meltdown, screaming at the technicians in the back of the room, "My f****ing slides are not working!" You could hear the techs scrambling to try to figure out how to fix the issue once again. By then, her energy was completely off, and she was no longer engaging with the crowd. She was flustered and nervously laughing while publicly humiliating the technicians, reminding the audience, "This is not my fault. The technicians need to do a better job for you guys." I had to follow that act and would need to change the energy of the crowd to make them forget about her presentation and her candor. *No pressure.*

She continued with this flustered and disjointed presentation while continuing to discredit the technicians who were feverishly trying to bring back the green screen. They just could not make it happen no matter what they tried. Welcome to the world of technology, where things fail at a moment's notice and you have to be ready to perform regardless of whether the lighting is bad, the microphone goes out, the slides are not uploaded, or you have a stain on your dress. After another 15 minutes of rambling, cursing, and blaming, the speaker simply walked off the stage and burst into the greenroom. The event coordinators followed and tried their best to apologize for the technical snafu.

I made my way up the stairs toward the stage, knowing that my job was a little bit more than my signature talk about confidence and women. I also had to bring back the trust of 7,000 people. I needed to feel their energy to win back their attention. I got on the stage, engaged them, made them laugh, and changed the mood for the rest of the day. Because the technicians still could not figure out how to get the green screens to reappear, I had to do my speech without any slides, but it didn't matter. I was ready.

After a heated exchange, the angry presenter and the coordinators rerecorded her session without an audience. I watched a completely different person who was calm, put together, and completely in her element. I thought, *If she could've tapped into her alter ego, this would have been smooth.* All that the audience would remember of this presenter was her poor demeanor under pressure.

Leadership does not give second chances. If that presentation was in a boardroom with decision makers, it would have been an immediate dismissal of any consideration to reach the C-suite. When you do not distance yourself from the learned behaviors of the past that feed your insecurities, you project onto an audience of strangers a person who is emotional and passively reacting to her fear. Alter egos are designed with these unexpected disasters in mind. They help you separate from the problem and act dispassionately. That is a sign of a leader worthy of the C-suite.

Benefits of an Alter Ego

Acts as a defense mechanism

Deters self-limiting language

Prevents overreacting or misinterpreting criticism

Encourages and cheerleads like a good friend

Helps detach from past patterns and fears

Enables you to realistically assess your performance, as your alter ego is less biased and self-critical

Guards against panic and is resilient in the face of the unknown

Four Steps to Create Your Alter Ego

I discovered the importance of the alter ego when I made the transition from corporate America to founding my own company. Many of the stories and labels I grew up with stuck with me in adulthood. As I began to shape my career and my future as a business leader, I had to consistently unlearn the labels that I was praised for wearing as a child. Unlearning a lifelong pattern of self-limiting beliefs is much harder than learning to appreciate your gifts and talents. Some of my unlearning was cultural, racial, spiritual, with a focus on ending heteronormative beliefs and stereotypes. I was conditioned to think that a woman's place was not to dream of becoming a high-powered business leader, but rather to become the assistant to the CEO. I had to consistently fight to unlearn these myths so that I could become the person I knew I could be. (We will deep dive into women stereotypes in the next chapter.)

The journey of transitioning from corporate America, with all of its safeties and perks, to building a company that advocates for women leaders in primarily male-dominated professions was not easy. Although I have worked my way to the C-suite to secure meetings with several high-power leaders, most of those meetings came as a result of speaking on prestigious stages across the world. The social proof and consistent follow-up to phone calls and emails are important; however, the most effective way to make connections with decision makers is to be in front of a room so you can highlight your value in the least amount of time. Many people ask me what it takes to be a successful speaker. What they don't realize is that vetting new business opportunities, my partnerships and collaborations, as well as creating value for reputable companies, came as a result of my alter ego. Without it, I couldn't successfully communicate my talents on stage. Now that you see how the alter ego has worked for me, here are the four steps to building your persona.

Step 1: Know Your Goals

When I started my business, I knew I wanted to work with high-achieving women, so the goal was to be in the presence of large groups and engage as consistently as possible. The next step was to get in front of women around the world. Speaking and networking have helped me to build my company much faster than those who are focused on logos and posting online. It's great to have a social media manager, but it's even better when you can make 50 major appearances every year, including some big media outlets, and get the same effect. My alter ego knows when to turn on and off, and it's well aware of the goal.

Set your goals early. Determine where you want to be in your career next year, then create an interaction plan to get there. An interaction plan is a list of people you need to begin connecting with, but with your alter ego present. It is your moment to shine and brag about yourself and your skills, which will help generate referrals and introductions that are in direct alignment with your goal. Last, ask someone you trust to hold you accountable while celebrating your milestones along the way.

Social media can be quite effective in its ability to reach more of your ideal connections worldwide, but it became evident to me that many of the women who were in my target audience were not engaging on a consistent level with social media. I have learned that most people in the C-suite are watching you, but they will never interact with you. I'm guilty of being one of those non-interactors. It's not that I have a persona on social media; rather I'm very cautious about "liking" or "sharing" people's status or commenting because my ideal audience is following. So to avoid one of my ideal clients following my 90-year-old uncle, who sometimes says a few inappropriate things on Twitter and Facebook, I often respond to him offline, rather than allow my brand to highlight our relationship in public.

Step 2: Mirror the Image

When you come from the world of law firms, you become accustomed to wearing dark colors such as navy blue, gray, black, and maroon. It is acceptable to be completely covered and as muted as possible. I have not met a lawyer to date who doesn't have at least 10 dark-colored suits in their wardrobe. When I entered the world of business, I was exposed to women who wore bright colors; after so many years of playing down my wardrobe, my new connections seemed almost flamboyant to me. I had to look the part though. My alter ego took me shopping so I could mirror the new audience I was engaging with. I invested in dresses and bright-colored suits; the demand for my business has never been the same.

There is an image component to your alter ego. While changing your appearance will not shift your confidence, doing so does relate to your alter ego. Think to yourself, Who do you want to look like? Who do you admire? Who's your ideal example of a confident woman? Who exemplifies where you want to be in the next stage of your career or business? Start looking at these people's appearance, considering the simplest of things like their nails, hair, or even the way they walk. Your alter ego has to exude a level of confidence that is unquestionable. To attract your ideal leadership opportunity, you have to look the part, not just have a great résumé. People invest in confidence, not just qualifications. You want them to believe in you, and see you, because visibility is a leading component in the C-suite. If they can't see you, they won't value you.

Step 3: Build the Personality Profile

I'm well-known for being a bit stern, but a very forward-thinking straight shooter. I wanted to be taken seriously from the time I started transitioning on this path, and I also wanted to avoid feeling like I was just another woman trying to break into real estate. I wanted to be taken seriously and be invited into rooms where high-powered mergers and acquisitions were taking place. The only way that is possible, especially when you don't have the background for the seat that you want to sit in, is to create the personality that accompanies your alter ego.

I read several books on mergers and acquisitions, shadowed some of the best mentors in the business, and leveled up my skills so that I would be prepared when it was time to finally take my rightful seat at the table. Even when I didn't understand the language, I created a personality that helped me bridge the gap between verbiage and relationships, which subsequently helped me understand the industry much better and therefore broker several introductions.

Even if you have to fake it until you make it, you need to adopt a personality profile for your alter ego that mirrors where you want to be. If you want to be considered for executive-level opportunities, you need to learn how to speak like an executive now, so you can insert yourself in conversations that need the qualifications only you offer. Think about how you want people to talk about you when you leave the room.

Consider the residual impact you will have when you communicate with specific decision makers and gatekeepers. Also, in creating your personality trait, think about the lasting impact you will leave on the people that you are going to lead. The one thing I have learned since building my company is that the same alter ego may not work with the team that you will be leading. As a leader, you're going to have another personality trait for your future employees or team.

What do you want your team to say about you when you're not in the room? Are you easy to work with but firm in your expectations? Are you someone who communicates orders effectively and clearly? Are you someone they can trust? The C-suite is about managing duality between the decision makers with whom you need to communicate and the team with which you need to build trust to get the job done.

Step 4: Walk the Walk

I'm not ashamed to admit that even when I didn't know, I pretended. Building a company is hard work, especially if you don't have access to specific relationships that help you grow. One thing I have learned over the last decade as a business leader is that everything is tied to relationships. The impression that you leave with one person becomes the introduction that person helps to navigate for growth in your career. You are only a few handshakes away from an opportunity that will change your life forever, but you have to walk the walk.

Even if you feel that your alter ego is not ready, communicating with any level of confidence will require you to walk the walk. You have to muster up the courage to separate yourself and empower your alter ego to do the work for you even if you don't feel that you are at your highest level. It is important to separate the two to mask your insecurities and to highlight your best attributes.

I have my days when I'm not there. In my real life, I'm an introvert and also quite moody. There are days I don't want to interact with anyone, much less smile or pretend to be friendly when that's not how I'm feeling. But I always remember that my purpose for building The Confidence Factor for Women is to support women every day. When your purpose is bigger than your pain or struggles, you walk differently. When I make the decision to take myself out of the equation, put on my best dress, remember why I'm doing this, and show up, I can separate my feelings from my life's work—then I walk the walk. There have been so many times when I struggled just to turn the camera on and post videos on social media, but I know there's someone out there who needs to hear an encouraging word during such a restless time in the world. So no matter what, your journey to the C-suite will require you to put your emotions aside, get dressed, think about the impact you want to leave with others, and start walking.

Before I developed my alter ego, I would say things like, "I can't start a business. No bank will ever lend me money because I'm a Black woman." I never even tried to approach a bank because I already had my mind made up that it would never invest in my vision. It is easy to become victimized by your own beliefs, especially if you do not go and confront them. Those without an alter ego live in a world filled with hearsay evidence to substantiate all of the risks they refused to take. Once I discovered how to build a shield to protect my personal feelings from my business persona, everything changed. All of the stereotypes in the world can't touch me now.

Women-Centered Stereotypes

How to Break Out of the "Norm"

KEY TAKEAWAY

According to *Fortune* Magazine, women made up only 7.4% of the Fortune 500 in 2020. Only 37 women are represented at the top.

Every woman has had an experience with the word *nice*. Whether you are not nice enough, are being too nice, or are debating if you were nice at a gathering or networking function—what is it about this four-letter word that continues to plague us? We constantly replay our actions on a daily, almost hourly basis, to ensure we were nice to everyone, from the mailroom staff to the reception clerk to the CEO. We've been conditioned to think that being "nice" is a prerequisite for our career success; thus we traditionally settle for less challenging professional paths such as clerical work and customer service, where being "nice" is an expectation. I have never said, "She's valuable because she's so nice." And the longer we are preoccupied with how women are "supposed" to act and negate how women should lead, the goalpost will continue to move away from the C-suite.

I have known "nice" women—many are my family and a few are my friends—who continue to struggle financially due to this "nice girl" syndrome. They're passed up for promotions and don't know what is preventing them from moving up the leadership ladder. It is not only the conditioning but the fact that they are willing to lower their expectations to accommodate their passive behavior while justifying their extreme ability to be nice at all times.

There's another four-letter word women contend with—*pink*. Come across any shade of the color, and people immediately perceive feminine qualities. When it comes to niceness and other stereotypical behavioral expectations, the pink perception is a gender-specific assumption about the lack of perceived intellect and go-getter aggressiveness of nice girls. Nice girls are less likely to speak up, so their silence is easily assumed to be a sign of limited input or valuable opinion. A nice girl has already sold herself on the lie that she should be happy to even have a job, or that if she works hard with her head down, someone will come along and give her a promotion because she does not cause any trouble. I am not discrediting the color pink, but rather the perception that pink implies when it comes to intelligent women who want more from their careers. However, the need to be nice must begin to change if you want more valuable and promotion-worthy opportunities that will allow stakeholders to take your contributions seriously.

Are you here for friendships or for your career? While I believe that you have to create some level of kinship at work, that is not the primary reason you make the sacrifice for 40 to 80 hours a week.

As referenced by Madeline Farber in *Fortune,* the gender wage gap starts to noticeably widen when women hit age 32, and women's pay decreases by nearly 20 percent of men's by age 40. A primary factor that contributes to the widening the gender equity gap at the age of 32 is women experiencing interruptions, such as starting or expanding their family or becoming the primary caregiver for an aging parent. In my company's surveys with our clients and other leaders we have worked with in the past, between the ages of 32 and 40, women assume their value has decreased due to the number of unplanned absences in their work history. When they return to work after the birth of a child or caring for an ailing parent, they frequently reenter at the same pay rate, or lower.

Women have second-guessed themselves out of the C-suite by creating false narratives about the value of their work due to personal absences. Last I checked, it was not a crime to give birth and expand your family. Besides, I do not think men would understand the strain that childbirth takes on the body postpartum. Yet, overwhelmingly, women discount this major life achievement and turn back to being "nice."

A study referenced in the Organizational Behavior and Human Decision Processes called "Social incentives for gender differences in the propensity to initiate negotations: Sometimes it does hurt to ask," states, "Conventional wisdom (e.g., 'it pays to ask' and 'the squeaky wheel gets the grease') suggests that, if women want the same resources and opportunities as men, then they should learn to seek out, rather than shy away from, opportunities to negotiate. . . . Women's reluctance as compared to men to initiate negotiations may be an important and underexplored explanation for the asymmetric distribution of resources, such as compensation, within organizations."

What Holds Women Back from Asking?

Every television show or political highlight that features a negotiation makes the act appear adversarial and highly emotional. Nothing could be further from the truth, especially if you're prepared to know what to ask for and when to ask for it. The reason why the nice girls never get the corner office is they simply don't ask for it. Being nice is an assumption that you are willing to be passive and forgo gratification in a gamble to be a "free" team player, rather than a valued member of a successful team. It conflates a personality type with value, whereby women who have been conditioned to focus more on their personality will forgo asking for their value because they're using someone else's negative experience to justify a potential outcome.

When we are defining the word *nice*, we are describing women who continue to perform in a childlike manner—compliant, passive, the Good Samaritan of the office, concerned about what people think of her, patient, and always pleasant.

Pink Professional Plague
The William and Mary School of Law published a white paper titled "Some Dumb Girl Syndrome: Challenging Destructive Stereotypes of Female Attorneys," which I reference in many of my talks. This 47-page research paper, authored by Ann Bartow, examines the historical journey of jurisprudence and the importance of the feminist movement

to change perceptions about female intellect and longevity in the hyper-male profession of law.

One of the most fascinating examples of the pink perception that was examined in the study was the 2001 movie *Legally Blonde*, which is based on a novel by Amanda Brown, where the lead character, Elle Woods, who is portrayed as a blonde woman of limited academic intellect, manages to score well on the LSAT and gain entry into Harvard Law School. The consistent characterization of pink throughout the movie continued to create a perception that Elle could never succeed as a trial attorney, but by the end, she managed to shift the narrative. However, the movie did more harm than good in creating an anti-intellectualism connection between successful women leaders and the color pink.

For instance, one of the male critics of the film which was referenced in the above mentioned study stated, "she [Elle Woods] has keen insights, which come from her life as a ditsy, clothes-mad, superficial and shallow woman and human being—someone whose idea of stress reduction is having her nails done. The movie does make fun of her, yes, but affectionately." Although *Legally Blonde* is a win in the world of cinematography, it does more harm than good as it continues to diminish the idea that well-qualified women can still wear pink and not be ditsy.

On the other hand, it reflects a part of a larger problem that we continue to face. That is, the idea that to understand what women want in the workplace, you must make it pink. The thought that the only dialect that we comprehend must be made in pink is insane, but it is part of a larger social construct. As a direct result, corporations have marginalized women from high-growth opportunities due to this pink perception. We have overcrowded specific professions, such as assistants, nursing, teaching, childcare, administrative professions, beauty, and fashion, to name a few. These professions have commonly attracted the pink perception, as they over-index by gender and are traditionally marketed toward women as stable career paths with predictable growth opportunities.

The perception is the association of pink with a lack of qualified intellect. The stigma that is placed on women by the presence of the color pink, primarily by powerful men, demotes women to a childlike standard of thought. Although I love the color pink myself, like many other women, its professional use—literally or symbolically—can lead to negative considerations of your value, especially when you are trying to communicate your value.

I never thought pink perception was real until I started my first company and used a bright shade of pink in my initial logo. My team sent out hundreds of prospecting materials to corporate stakeholders to commence exploratory conversations about leadership training and research. All of the responses were lowball offers. It was quite frustrating, and there were moments when I was about to give up until I received a call from a branding agent who saved my company from a path to insolvency.

I will call her "Kelly." Kelly called me one morning from an executive branding firm that worked with a few of my biggest idols. It was a sales call, of course, but she gave me advice about how to make some major changes. I decided to hire her firm, and a few days later, I was on a plane flying to Los Angeles.

Kelly said, "Do you know why you are attracting an avalanche of lowball offers?"

"Because my pitch deck needs work?" I guessed.

"It's not your pitch deck," Kelly explained. "It's your pink pitch deck."

"What do you mean?"

"All of the pink calligraphy is killing your credibility and making your company appear unqualified. You can represent feminism and avoid the pink professional plague."

It was my aha moment of transformation.

We sat in her office, brainstorming ideas on branding my company, which caters to the advancement of women but must get through male gatekeepers. It dawned on me that Kelly had finally helped me break through my own pink beliefs. I realized that I was conditioned to normalize separation of men and women.

Think about it for a moment:

When a man is a doctor, he is a doctor.

When a woman is a doctor, we refer to her as a "female" doctor.

When a man is a chef, he is a chef.

When a woman is a chef, we refer to her as a "female" chef.

When a man is a business owner, he just owns a successful business.

When a woman is a business owner, she is a "female" business owner.

We communicate gender as an adjective of a profession as a way to formalize the use of pink, even today. It is a silent whistle that the value of the collaborative is discounted and labeled as one of the pink pomp-and-circumstance business models.

Kelly and I developed a pitch deck that was gender neutral yet conveyed a heavy emphasis on gender inclusion. I eliminated all of the pink shades from my marketing collateral, and male stakeholders began to listen to our presentation without the need to put us in that stereotypical pretty pink box of "frilly" games.

I recently had a fascinating conversation with Rohini Dey, owner of Vermilion Restaurants and guest on The Food Network, who told me, "It's time for women to get out of the pink cages and get into the ownership side of leadership." Essentially, we do not need to remain on the pink side of the line for it to be feminine.

Pink: A Safer Choice?

Women start businesses at a record level globally but often operate survival-level business models—high-overhead, low-profit-margin businesses such as hair salons, coaching or consulting, small or solo law firms, boutiques, daycare centers, bookkeeping, and so on that attract the pink stigma. On the other hand, men start companies such as Facebook, Tesla, Amazon, Microsoft, and Apple, using successful high-profit-margin business models. These business models are scalable and attract investors to inflate the value. In the meantime, although a few women-owned companies have reached unicorn status, many are riddled with challenges, primarily with funding.

Women also apply for survival-level careers and jobs, such as receptionist, teacher, assistant to the CEO, paralegal, human resources and HR management, staffing executive, nursing, and so on. Although all of the mentioned careers are well respected, they are considered "women-centered" professions, which also fit within the pink perception of career choices. I believe many of these professions are intentionally marketed to women to continue to feed the value gap that keeps women highly underpaid. I have given talks several times for the Society for Human Resource Management, and every time I stand onstage, there are thousands of women in the audience. Nursing is also a profession that is in high demand, and all of the educational advertisers create ads that feature women, mostly single mothers, who are looking to transition to a high-paying career. If you don't believe me, Google nursing programs and watch the ads. Or, even better, ask yourself how many times you noticed or said, "male nurse," and thought it was a bit odd.

Additionally, Education Connection commercials always feature a struggling mother looking for a better career choice. The marketing plot is intentional as a way to continue the pink perception that "certain" jobs and business models are for women. Everything else is for men.

The pink perception has created socioeconomic norms and expectations, which have also impacted the wealth and equity gap for women, who continue to earn less than men, on average, and have continued to fall within the spectrum of career and business choices that have limited upward mobility. I struggled with this reality myself as an early graduate, as I was not taught how the pink perception would limit my growth and ability to communicate beyond my pink thought process. We have normalized specific professions as being more appropriate for women, which causes us to not communicate outside of our comfort zone.

Subsequently, we are most vulnerable to communicating with people who share common professional traits and attributes, which has conditioned us to fear stepping out of the pink box. There is a major deficit in high-level leadership positions, which if improved, the benefit will trickle down to all women. According to *Fortune*, at the time of this book, we only have a disappointing 7 percent presence in Fortune 500 CEO roles. Only 37 women are represented at the top, and although it is growing marginally, the numbers continue to reflect our fears and lack of confidence in asking for opportunities outside of our norms.

How the Nice Girl Perpetuates the Pink Perception

Well, quite simply, nice girls don't ask . . . for much. In 2004, Dr. Lois Frankel wrote the book *Nice Girls Don't Get the Corner Office*, which discusses the societal pressure of women in the workplace to be "nice" and "liked," rather than be respected, which could negatively impact their career. One of the inherent traits of a "nice girl" that was addressed in the book was smiling even when you are not happy, which is in itself one of the nonverbal forms of communication that create long-term limitations for women.

We smile because we have been conditioned that it is pleasing to others and it avoids any offensive gender-specific stereotyping. We walk past a colleague at work, we smile. We walk past a decision maker in the office who recites abhorrent statements against a coworker, we smile. We smile even when we are experiencing intense emotional pain. We have perfected smiling as a way to adhere to the childlike teachings that have conditioned us to be "pretty and well behaved."

How many times has a man passed you and said, "smile," and it made you smile? I used to feel like a little girl with my hair in twin ponytails as my grandfather used to take me to the candy store and the cashier would say, "Smile, pretty girl." I was so bashful, but I wanted the cashier to tell my grandad only good things about me. I always thought that by being nice, I would be rewarded.

When I entered the workplace in my twenties, I smiled daily.

- I smiled while I was being underpaid.
- I smiled while I was being disrespected consistently as male attorneys would often say, "You speak so well for a Black woman."
- I smiled as a difficult client called me the day after I gave birth to my son and fired me because I could not call him back in time because I was in the hospital.
- I smiled when I asked my supervisor if I could play some music at my desk and she responded, "as long as it's not gangsta rap." (Not all Black people listen to rap, by the way).
- I smiled when I asked for a raise and I was offered a whopping 4 percent, which was an extra $1,400 per year, and I was scared to reject the offer due to the fear of losing my job.

- I smiled when my supervisor told me that I could not eat at my desk because I chose to forgo my lunch hour to finish school, so eating anything throughout the day was cause for a write-up.

My beautiful, albeit passive smile was communicating my paralyzing complacency. I wore it as a badge of honor to express my deep sense of gratefulness to just keep my "foot in the door at work," while barely keeping the lights on at home. I anesthetized my pain by feeding myself the story of "be happy that you at least have a job," as I was underpaid, overworked, and emotionally abused by both my supervisors and myself.

In diagnosing my past issues with the "nice girl" syndrome, although I disagreed with most of the workplace politics, I subliminally used nonverbal cues to avoid conflict, which made me look agreeable. I specifically remember one instance at a law firm, when my office manager chased me down a hallway to ask me to stop wearing perfume because a few of the other women in the office did not like it. I was young, indecisive, and unsure if standing up to her would negatively impact my role, or lead to termination. With a smile on my face, and without inquiring why she was saying this to me, I graciously replied, "Sure, no problem," even though I never wore perfume. When I went back to my department, my supervisor could instantly sense a change in my demeanor. I shared the details of the encounter, and she started composing an email. I'm not sure what she said in the email, but within an hour, I was issued an apology.

You may be suffering with the same level of insecurity if:

- You have a difficult time saying no
- You use nonverbal communicators such as smiling and laughing to avoid mischaracterizations

- You overcommit your time
- You are worried about your team or coworkers more than your senior-level success and professional ambitions
- You do not negotiate annually
- You take constructive criticism personally
- You don't want to be labeled as "aggressive" or "a bitch"
- You apologize frequently
- You avoid difficult conversations
- You want to be liked and praised by everyone in the office
- You overthink everything
- You second-guess your own decisions
- You don't want to leave your current job because you care too much about your coworkers
- You are constantly thinking of the worst-case scenario
- You are invested in perfectionism
- You are worried about your appearance more than the quality of your work
- You use your mild-mannered, childlike voice when complimented by senior-level leaders
- You live for validation and approval from others
- You don't speak up in meetings due to the fear of not knowing or not having the right answer
- You do not make suggestions for new and innovative ways to increase productivity

I can go on and on, but I want it to sink in for a moment. How many times have you used nonverbal cues to agree or settle for less than you deserved simply because you are fixated on being "nice"? The pink perception has created a lasting stigma that you will accept any decision made because you do not want to change your gentle and kind demeanor. Instead, you still play office politics with other women, who have the same fears, while gossiping amongst yourselves, but never speak up or make your opinions heard.

I know why it is difficult to break an inherited cycle of compliance with the pink perception. You don't want to lose your job! It is better to "put up with it" than to change it. But if I can take a deeper dive for a moment, it is the story of our lives outside of work as well. We "put up" with numerous circumstances—dysfunctional friendships, toxic family members, and even overbearing domestic relationships. My cousin and I recently reminisced about our grandmother. My cousin said, "Granny used to tell me that I had to learn how to put up with a few things, even a few extramarital issues, if I want to marry, so I never got married."

I responded, "Are there any women who would be willing to put up with that today?"

As we laughed it off as a memory, I knew that infidelity is an issue for women, and in some cultures, it is an accepted norm. I remember watching the 2017 hit movie, *Girls Trip*, where the lead character, Ryan Pierce, played by Regina Hall, was working hard to keep her image as the nice girl to her followers and friends while dealing with infidelity in her personal life. There were moments throughout the movie where she continued to admit that she was "putting up" with it for the benefit of her career while calling it "an agreement."

I don't want to get too deep, but by now you understand the high tolerance of the unlimited boundaries of nonverbal communication, and the enormous pressure women endure to continue to keep at least one "foot in the door." We have also adopted such internalized pressure because we are risk-averse. If you have ever played the childhood game musical chairs, you may understand why we have an adverse reaction to the slightest form of risk. Getting a seat when the music cuts off is the idea of the game. If you get a seat, you are safe. If not, everyone in the room starts laughing at you. I remember questioning if the objective of the game is to always have a seat or to avoid a room full of onlookers laughing at you. For the most part, it depends on your level of sensitivity.

The conditioning to be nice happened in childhood. For me, the pink perception was perpetuated in grade school! As girls, the stories we read focused on grabbing the hearts of Prince Charming, dreaming of our wedding day, a white picket fence in the suburbs, and hosting dinner parties and social events for the community. Most of our thoughts were not directed toward high professional ambitions and standards. Instead, we became accustomed to applying for roles that fit a feminine norm: secretary, assistant to the CEO, receptionist, pastry chef, childcare worker or nanny, or a homemaker and housewife. I knew how to cook before I knew how to read because my grandmother and aunts used to fly to the United States from Trinidad every summer and show all of the girls in our family how to clean peas and boil rice properly. We were conditioned to do well in school as a backup plan, not primarily as a path to success.

Although academia has leveled the playing field a bit, until my freshman year in university, teachers constantly tried to tame my ambitions and consistently asked me to be "realistic." When I was in the seventh grade, my teacher, Mrs. Mamby, asked everyone to stand up and tell the class what we wanted to become when we grew up. Many of the boys said "firefighter," "astronaut," "the president of the United

States," and "a doctor." The girls started with "a nurse," "a teacher," "a mom," "a secretary." When it was my turn, I said, "a federal judge." The class erupted in a round of laughter that shattered my confidence to my core. Mrs. Mamby looked at me and said, "Come on sweetie, think of something else and be realistic. When you come to class tomorrow, think about what you want to be."

The next day, when Mrs. Mamby asked me for an answer, I said "I'm sorry, I want to be a teacher." She smiled and said, "That's better!" I only said it to avoid the bullying and the potential of Mrs. Mamby calling my grandmother. We were practically neighbors. I didn't want to seem defiant or forceful, so I folded and lowered my standards to avoid future judgment. The following year, for the eighth grade, the school automatically placed me in an elective that shifted my perspective—home economics. It felt like brainwashing, as I had to learn how to make chop suey, chicken tikka masala, and coq au vin for a qualifying grade for high school. I attended a small private school, so there was nowhere to run or other electives to take. The boys were moved to sports science to learn how to coach sports teams.

Everywhere I turned, I was taught to stop being "so ambitious" and learn how to "be realistic," "share," and "think of others before you think of yourself." These messages are generational in our learning institutions and media. In his book *The Triple Bind*, Stephen Hinshaw explains that as girls reach adolescence, they are increasingly asked to conform to what he views as "an impossible set of standards." Girls are also taught to focus on empathy and other people's feelings instead of their own. Hence, we are conditioned to choose professions that focus on the common good of others, instead of ourselves, and we apologize if we set the bar too high.

Become a "Nasty" Woman

Everyone has a breaking point.

Do you remember where you were in 2009 when Kanye West interrupted Taylor Swift as she accepted the MTV award for Best Video by a Female Artist? It was Taylor Swift's first award as a freshman artist to the MTV Awards circuit. She started her speech with the most thankful and humble round of acknowledgments, which was going quite well until Kanye West walked up those stairs and stole her spotlight.

At first, I thought that it was an intro to her performance, so I dismissed it as innocent until I watched both Taylor Swift and Beyoncé shudder, wide-eyed. Taylor could not seem to get her focus back, which was completely understandable. The crowd began expressing their displeasure with Kanye, as he boastfully shouted, "Imma let you finish, but Beyoncé had the best video of all time!"

I called a close friend after that, and we jokingly shared what we would have done if we were in that moment. I am sure Taylor Swift did not plan for her first acceptance speech to be interrupted on live television, nor by a fellow musician. But the fact that her reaction was nonverbal, non confrontational, and seemingly polite and poised speaks more to the expectation of being "nice" than ensuring your voice is heard.

The Taylor Swift of today is not the same as the one in 2009. Her speech during the award show, or lack thereof, represents a long history of women, who are constantly interrupted. An article in the *New York Times*, by Susan Chira titled "The Universal Phenomenon of Men Interrupting Women," stated that interruptions are "nearly a universal experience for women when they are outnumbered by men."

Although I would like to think this is solely a men versus women issue, it is false. Senior-level women interrupt junior and freshman-level women as well, which creates the same level of intimidation.

In a 2015 editorial by Sheryl Sandberg and Adam Grant in the *New York Times,* "Speaking While Female," Sandberg states, "When a woman speaks in a professional setting, she walks a tightrope. Either she's barely heard or she's judged as too aggressive. When a man says virtually the same thing, heads nod in appreciation for his fine idea." In my experience, this is the communication stumbling block that women encounter—finally managing to find the courage to speak up for themselves, only to be interrupted and discounted publicly for their contribution.

Let's talk about getting over this hurdle.

1. **Speak to your manager or HR manager.** This is the only way to ensure that your company deliberately implements a universal policy around supporting all voices within the company. Make sure that you document the conversation and follow up with your suggestions in writing.

   Hi (Name),

   I just wanted to express some concerns about my observation in our last quarterly meeting on Monday. We have fourteen women on our team, and only three spoke up during the meeting, and I believe the other women did not feel included.

   Can we implement a universal system, where we go around the room and ask everyone about their input for the quarter as a way to take the pressure off of those who are not as confident about speaking up?

   Thanks,

2. **Finish your point!** So someone interrupted you. Make sure you continue to finish your point. Finish what you started and do not allow the meeting to continue without your complete thought.

   Thanks for clarifying my thoughts ahead of me, John. So to further substantiate my point about this month's performance report, we have a 43 percent surplus, which I believe can be used next quarter to generate bonuses.

3. **Stand up!** Stand up when you are speaking. Even if it is the tradition to sit around the table and discuss workplace issues and performance, stand up and redirect the focus of the room toward you. (Call upon your alter ego if necessary.) This will improve your posture, tone, and confidence. Most of all, people are less likely to believe that you are a "nice girl" who holds her head down at work. It will be a memorable moment where your colleagues and decision makers will view you as an asset.

4. **Don't backpedal.** Now is not the time to start using defeating opening lines when speaking. Audit your language before you speak. Remember, your presence is valuable and intentional. Never start with:

   - *"I'm sorry to interrupt, but . . ."*
   - *"I don't mean to be rude, but . . ."*
   - *"Can I say something please?"*
   - *"I respectfully disagree, because . . ."*
   - *"I don't know if this is worth anything, but . . ."*

Never apologize before you speak. It shows your weakness as a leader, and you will be vulnerable to interruption. Speak with authority, even if it scares you. The fear will subside the moment you start speaking.

5. **Become an ally.** Even if you do not have anything to add to a meeting, you can support the other women who do. If you see other women being interrupted or intimidated, support them. Help them find the courage to speak up and remind them to avoid apologizing at all costs. Remind them to stand up and celebrate their bravery. There is power in alliances.

   Please allow Rosa to finish her point. You continue to interrupt her every time she speaks, and it is quite rude, and especially detrimental to the good of the team. Rosa is an excellent team leader, and her contribution is valuable to achieving our sales goals this month.

6. **Join your local Toastmasters.** I have heard the old tale that public speaking is the number one fear of most people in the world; however, it is a crucial skill, especially in meetings. Speaking with your colleagues and friends is not a challenge, but moving the same message in front of an audience with various views is challenging.

   Joining your local Toastmasters is a great way to sharpen your communication skills in front of an audience while gaining valuable feedback on how to improve. Meetings will allow you to learn about tone, owning a room, pivoting a point, and how to sharpen your vocabulary to make your point relevant. Remember, you cannot avoid verbal communication as a leader. Effective communication requires a mix of strategies, but verbal communication is always most effective.

7. **Stop overpracticing!** When you overpractice or overprepare, it is easy to negatively self-assess your performance. The best preparation is relaxation. The more you

practice, the more flaws you will find, and there is a likelihood that doubt will set in.

Relax, breathe in, unwind your mind, and imagine yourself standing up to add value in a meeting. Practice doesn't always make perfect. It can make your fears worse.

Communicating in a Crisis

The Difference Between Reaction and Response

KEY TAKEAWAY

Passive communication is conditioned in women and takes many forms, including emotional reaction. Learning the art of the professional response is a key building block to gaining power.

My gray 1988 Honda Accord was parked at the corner of my block, when at around 2 a.m., its alarm sounded off. A man had slammed his car into my precious automobile, the only thing I owned, a source of autonomous pride in my fledgling adulthood. I was still living with my grandparents, but that Honda reminded me I was on my way. My grandmother, startled by the noise as well, stood by the window and watched as I ran down to the street leading a commotion of nosy, sleepy neighbors gathering around the scene of the accident.

I asked the driver of the car to hand me his insurance and registration, but he refused to respond to my request. Channeling my inner traffic cop, I requested again and again, "license and registration," and each time he refused, I became angrier. I finally bellowed, "Hand me your f****ng license and registration now!"

My grandmother clutched the windowsill, called me to the door, and with her proper English accent said, "Carol Callender, you must immediately walk up to the gentleman and apologize for your vile language. Mrs. Pierce, Mrs. Paul, and Mr. Anderson are all watching, and your language was highly inappropriate. After you apologize to him, walk up to all of their windows and apologize for your behavior."

There was no dispute with my grandmother; I followed her instructions. When the police arrived, I realized that the gentleman was not speaking because he was scared. I hadn't considered his fear. Instead his silence had spun me into an emotional state, causing me to react to what I perceived as lack of concern or responsibility. My perception had clouded my response, and I had reacted hastily.

Although at the time I did not agree with my grandmother's approach, because her motive was to save face and adhere to her cultural practice of respect for our elders, she was right. Besides, she was not a reactive person. My grandmother communicated in a carefully crafted and thought-out way. She used to take days to write carefully drafted letters that read more like novels to her sisters abroad. She included so much depth and description of her everyday experiences so her sisters could feel like they were living with her. In no way was my grandmother a confrontational person, and she consistently tried to show us the importance of avoiding reaction to every situation. It's the reason why I never had any fights in high school and avoided most of the conflicts that some of the kids in our community got into.

Today, as a leader, I have learned the negative consequences of reacting to situations hastily. I've also learned that there is a major difference between reaction and response. Many times I have to walk away from social media to avoid reacting to a negative comment on Twitter or a negative critique of one of my videos on TikTok. I do my best to avoid engaging in highly emotional, and often adversarial, conversations that can potentially harm my career. It takes years of discipline to identify why instead of taking a moment to breathe and carefully respond in a manner that can highlight our growth and leadership abilities, we take the low road of emotional reaction. I also believe that age and maturity are predominant factors in avoiding reactive responses. The older I become, the less conflict I need in my life, so I choose which conversations I will react to and which I will respond to.

The Emotional Element of Communication

According to Kendra Cherry in an article titled "Emotions and Types of Emotional Responses," published by VeryWell Mind.com, an emotion is a complex state that involves three distinct components: a subjective experience, a physiological response, and a behavioral or expressive response. Understanding emotion in this way has helped me see more clearly the escalating stages of my emotions when faced with challenging moments.

A subjective experience is the most personal of the three components. It suggests that there is no universal emotion for universal situations, such as death, nervousness, or fear. Everyone experiences each situation in a unique way, and subjective personal factors will impact each one's emotional response. This is why some people in a situation after a heated meeting might behave very differently.

A physiological response is where we get our "fight or flight" reactions to emotions such as fear or danger. The physiological response varies, but the most common are trembling, sweat, screaming, or even running. You might have experienced the feeling of lightheadedness or literally a heated head after the president of the company announces no bonuses for the year or a round of layoffs to come.

The behavioral response is the one most common in the workplace, where we express our emotions and interpret cues from others, such as colleagues and friends. Our response is based on their behavior. It can also affect our body language and communication style and clarity.

Emotions can impact your mood at work and you may feel:

- Short-tempered
- Stressed
- Limited concentration
- Inability to focus
- Unable to clearly express your thoughts
- Joy
- Fear
- Happiness

Discerning between a reaction and a response is based on emotion. Emotional communicators allow external factors to impact their mood, performance, and communication style. Throughout the next few pages you'll discover which communication style you display at work and understand the significance of how you respond to your colleagues, gate-keepers, and clients. Keep in mind that as women, we are naturally more emotional than our male colleagues; however, it can impact our productivity and performance.

High-level leaders are aware of the power of an effective response and have practiced avoiding reaction. Many leaders go as far as retaining crisis managers to respond to criticism or any inappropriate reactions that could impact their role. Most of us must act as our own crisis management teams, remaining in control of how others perceive our value. We must have agency over our communication style and move from reactive to responsive.

Reactive Communication

Have you ever been in a store or stopped through a fast-food restaurant to pick up a quick drink and felt negative energy from the clerk? And their energy causes you to change your energy? Subsequently, instead of maintaining your pleasant demeanor, you react negatively, and then the experience changes. In the world of customer service, I've always believed that some of the negative comments and reviews on websites such as Yelp are only a result of reactive communication, firing off a comment in the moment without any processing, just pure emotion, with motives based on something negative like revenge, righteous indignation, or an ego bruise. As the old saying goes, *two wrongs don't make it right.* But I admit I have been guilty of falling into the same trap, especially when I was in my twenties. If people looked at me the wrong way, I would look at them the wrong way. This roller coaster of reactive communication, in both verbal and nonverbal forms, can negatively impact your professional candor. It doesn't matter who changed your demeanor, you will always be seen as the antagonist. Sometimes, reactive communication could be the result of getting to the office late due to heavy traffic, your personal life, or maybe that's just who you are—either way, negativity does not work at work.

When I think back to the beginning of the popularity of social media, I made some major mistakes by overpersonalizing my responses to negative feedback. For many years, I avoided placing a profile picture on Facebook and Twitter because I had issues with body dysmorphia, and I was quite concerned about being the face of my own company. It took two to three years for me to get over my angst over my appearance. Before I became the face of my company, I had been comfortable and accustomed to the anonymity an office provides; suddenly out on my own, I became highly critical of my appearance and it took a toll on my emotions. With the popularity of social media driving the necessity to have an internet presence for my company to gain social validation for growth, I had to work on my self-confidence issues and take a risk.

The day that I removed the veil of random stock pictures of cute animals from my profile on both platforms, I left myself susceptible to immediate criticism—the same criticism I was working so hard to avoid became the criticism I had to read in the threads. Some people were shocked that I was Black, and others were surprised that I was a full-sized woman. The comments varied, but for some reason, I only focused on the negative reactions. I fed into their negativity and reacted impulsively and immaturely. Some people called me chunky and freckled-faced, to which I fired off, "and so is your mother!" I made a few other comments that I am not proud of, but I was reacting—perhaps overreacting. My motivation was to make my aggressors feel the same hurt and low self-esteem that I felt when I read their comments. And the more they continued to react, the worse it became for me. I was defensive, and I wanted to inflict the same pain that was done to me, with no regard for my brand or what I wanted my company to stand for.

Meanwhile, I ignored all of the gracious compliments from people who were in full support of finally viewing the face behind the name. If there were 500 comments, I spent most of my time responding to the 40 negative messages, instead of remaining thankful and mindfully responding to the 460 positive comments.

Once I accepted that success is always accompanied by harsh and unsolicited criticism, I learned how to ignore the negativity that social media invites. Today, when I write articles for various magazines, sometimes my Twitter feed is filled with hate-filled reactions to my opinions; nevertheless, I do not react, because I know the never-ending sinkhole it will suck me into. Practically speaking, reacting to everything takes up time, unproductive time that you can never reclaim. It feels validating in the moment to "get someone back" or to defend and guard yourself against negative feedback, but the time that you spend trying to find the best comeback line or statistic to back you up can be better spent with silence and contemplation to determine why you are so bothered in the first place. This is how we grow, not by resorting to "yo mama" jokes.

Although reactive people may look strong, dominant, and confident, they are acting quite passively. For example, when I reacted to some of my social media critics by stating "and so is your mother," I wanted the aggressor to feel my emotional pain, instead of taking the high road and ignoring the comment or responding with a positive statement. It is a passive approach that can be perceived as immature, instead of professional. Reactive responses and communication are emotional character flaws we all have that are predicated on an external trigger. In your career or business, it is seen as a sign of weakness and shortsightedness. When you react to something, you are simply seeking a reaction. Also, there is nothing to gain from a reactive response. The best example is road rage—there are few winners in a road rage war, just expletives and hand gestures. Some people just want a reaction out of you. In the office, reactive people believe that this personality type is an effective way to communicate their strengths. But decision makers are well aware of the negative impact reactivity can have on the success of the company. They know the difference between a reaction and a response:

Reaction	Response
Emotionally driven	Requires emotional intelligence
Based in fear	Shows self-awareness and self-regulation
About the moment	Considers the long-term goal

A few members of my husband's family are in the retail business, and they have to monitor their employees to ensure they don't communicate reactively to tough customers. A few years ago, they had one employee, whom we'll call "Bob," who was in charge of the morning openings. In retail, sometimes you have angry customers who say inappropriate things to the cashier or manager. But it's the job of the clerk to mitigate the mood, not exasperate it. However, Bob was feeding into the negativity of some of the customers, and the owners started losing revenue. My in-laws installed cameras behind the register to find out how Bob was engaging with some of their regular patrons—and they were shocked by his aggressive and reactive tone. They had to dismiss Bob and rebuild their loyal customer base to keep the store in business.

The most common situations that elicit a reactive response in the workplace are:

- Pressure from supervisors or managers about deadlines
- Interactions with difficult people in the office
- Anxiety or nervousness
- Disappointments, setbacks, humiliation, and discouragement
- Working in a hostile environment
- Being overworked and underappreciated
- Adverse interactions with other team members
- Feeling ostracized or alienated from the team
- Personal issues
- Financial stress

Your career will always be a series of interactions and engagements with people, and there's no way around it. A reactive person responds negatively to people, while creating friction. Answering emotionally, angrily, or petulantly (walking off during a conversation, speaking loudly, becoming animated during a conversation), are signs of reaction in professional correspondence. You cannot escape the chain of people who are connected to your success in the C-suite; learning to accept what you cannot control and responding in ways that illustrate that you are in control of yourself and what needs to happen moving forward is a distinct attribute of leaders. As I shared with you in an early chapter about the importance of developing an alter ego, it is easy to combat all of your reactions by creating a layer of defense between who you are and your character at work. It will also help you fight the natural adrenalized urge to react to specific situations.

Reactiveness is an immature emotional response. For example, if toddlers ask for a toy they want in a store, and the parent refuses, some children may throw a temper tantrum. Public temper tantrums can be quite an ordeal for any parent—from children stomping on the floor to screaming at the top of their lungs, they take an emotional toll on the parent. Also, the parent is worried about how their child's behavior looks to others. My son did this in the supermarket once when he was three years old, and I will never forget the embarrassment as he screamed, "Mommy, I want my Lightning McQueen, Mommy, I want my Lightning McQueen now!" as he demanded a toy at the top of the freezer aisle, which happened to match a toy he had in his room. It is hard to punish a child for a temper tantrum because their behavior reflects an emotional connection to something. It is the same thing with being reactive. Decision makers recognize that you are emotionally connected with a specific outcome, and your reactiveness is a reflection of your impatience. But if you have no self discipline in how you communicate, your professional journey is on the line. Although many people view this level of defensiveness and sometimes aggression to be positive, once you are deemed difficult to work with, it will work against you.

Keep in mind:

- The reaction is impulsive and emotional
- Reactiveness is not factually based; it is based on assumptions and feelings that arise out of fear
- The reaction is a defense mechanism against something
- You risk being deemed difficult to work with and ostracized from high-level opportunities
- A reaction does not take into account why the person is engaging with you in that way (Like when my precious Honda was slammed into, and I didn't care or consider that the man was scared over what he'd done.)

How to Become Less Reactive

Recognize your triggers. Reactive communicators must be aware of their triggers. Whether it's a person whom you may feel is abrasive or personal issues in your life, it is important to document everything that causes you to react impulsively.

Make a plan. Next, create a plan to minimize or avoid the trigger, while practicing effective responses, which I will cover in the next section. Once you create a guided template to navigate specific verbal or nonverbal interactions, you will build a new, less defensive rapport with your colleagues.

Pause before responding. It's best for you and your career to take as much time as you need before reacting to any scenario. You can always feel your anxiety approaching. For example, let's say your trigger is your team leader, whose email each morning with a list of demands immediately changes your mood. Take a moment to breathe.

The moment you begin to respond to the email, you will press the backspace tab to retract all of your emotionally personalized replies. Instead, respond with a brief affirmative tone to avoid subsequent follow-up correspondence.

For example, a nonreactive reply is:

The report will be forwarded before the end of the day.
Thank you.

The opening line of a response to a request or email from someone you view as assertive or aggressive is important. Avoid opening lines such as:

- *Per my last email*
- *As I stated earlier*
- *Kindly refer to . . .*

Such statements are aggressive communication starters because the recipient can perceive their tone as patronizing, passive-aggressive, or insubordinate (which we covered in Chapter 2). When it comes to decision makers, whether we like it or not, it matters how they perceive and receive our messages.

Think long term. Where do you want to be in your professional career in 5 or 10 years? Keep in mind, you must communicate your way to the top. Reactive communicators are short-term thinkers who may not be thinking of a career. However, ambitious thinkers know the value of relationships, even with difficult people.

You can't run from difficult people, but you are in control of your energy and how you respond to others in the workplace. Avoid adversarial encounters that could activate your defensive trigger. Always think about the long-term impact on your career—one reaction could change everything.

Start Responding!

I was recently invited to a discussion with Sheryl Sandberg, COO of Facebook and cofounder of Lean In. It was based on a joint report, *The State of Black Women in Corporate America*, published by Lean In and McKinsey & Company, on improving workplace policies to focus on the advancement of Black women. I was honored to be a part of the discussion for an op-ed I was drafting for *Inc.* magazine. While it was the first time Sheryl and I discussed diversity on a deep level, this was my second time connecting with her.

Sheryl possesses such passion and care regarding the topic of advancing women to the C-suite. In a moment of excitement, I shared a snippet of the interview with a journalist group on Facebook. I was beaming, because not only did I have a private interview with Sheryl, but I received an advance copy of the report before its release, which allowed me to create additional content from the statistics.

I posted the link to the interview in the Facebook group, which was filled with mature, accomplished writers; I expected a few negative antics, but nothing major. One gentleman responded to my post in record time. Below is a transcript of our exchange:

My post:

I was honored to have a moment today to sit and chat with Sheryl Sandberg about how to create inclusive policies for Black women.

This is only a preview of our conversation. Stay tuned. Tomorrow, it will be the first story in Inc. magazine titled, "The State of Black Women in Corporate America."

His reply:

Great! How about asking her what she's doing to combat misinformation on FB in time for the election? She's indirectly hurting people of color by FBs indifference.

My reply:

You are more than welcome to contact her office for an interview to get all of the answers to your questions. That was not the purpose of mine.

His reply:

I hear you and I appreciate that. I don't expect to minimize your joy and getting Sheryl Sandberg's attention on your work and I applaud you for your efforts. I just believe Sheryl is another leader we fanboy or fangirl over because of how she has made it and learned it when in reality she's made millions if not billions in systems that she doesn't want to take responsibility for.

My response:

Thank you for remembering not to minimize my joy, I am appreciative. I don't believe in fanning anyone as I have been fortunate to sit with world leaders far more successful than her. I had a specific agenda and specifically targeted questions based on a joint report with McKinsey & Company. There is a time and place for politics, which is not why I sought this interview for my content and column.

His reply:
You're amazing Carol. I didn't mean to minimize your efforts. We need people like you and hey I also coach at companies that are problematic. I may not be a fan of them but I am a fan of you. Please keep up the great work.

It took an army of strength to take the high road in this conversation and avoid the emotional reaction, where I wanted to tell him which rock he could go under. A clear response to the post was necessary, but I also needed to reflect a high level of professionalism, as I was aware of the amount of attention this post would receive. The moderator of the group praised the interaction as he stated, "It could have gone another way, but you both found common ground."

This is a classic example of someone diminishing the progress of another in return for attention—and from someone who has extreme views on issues yet is unable to confront them in a proper context. It happens frequently, and if you are vulnerable to public critique, responding too fast may result in a personal or emotional reaction, which is exactly what this critic expected. Hence, as I was highlighting the issue of equality for women, he attempted to use this moment to deflect to politics. By taking a moment to refrain from taking the bait, I was able to think carefully about my response.

The following is a breakdown of how I thought through my response process:

You are more than welcome to contact her office for an interview to get all of the answers to your questions.
That was not the purpose of mine.

I needed a few hours to avoid reacting to his post and to make this line as short, clear, and direct as possible. I wanted to be clear that the purpose of my interview was not germane to his anger with Facebook's policies. Also, I wanted to be clear that my interview was in direct alignment with my business, therefore, I was not the best person to answer his concerns about Facebook's policies, but there was an open-door policy for him to request an interview.

There is a time and place for politics, which is not why I sought this interview for my content and column.

In this part of the third response, which also took several hours to reply to, I directed his attention to my UVP (unique value proposition). My column specializes in women in the workplace, which was highlighted in my description of the post. However, the responder continued to use his time to create an attack over a broader narrative, which was unrelated to the interview. Although he may or may not have a valid issue, I wanted to ensure he engaged his anger toward the institution of the platform, rather than using my achievement as a pawn.

The key to a clear response, rather than a reaction, is to remain germane to your position. This is the primary reason the responder was forced to subliminally apologize for his assertions in his response because it was not in direct relation to my interview and his attempt at publicly positioning an issue that was irrelevant to the interview was quickly grounded.

More importantly, the response to this post, and *yes, it is still up on FB*, was an attempt to distract, defer, and discredit my work in public. It was reaction bait, and he thought it would anger me enough to be rewarded with a personal attack. It is a disturbing trend that intentionally rewards people for negativity and public disgrace, and it is something you must prepare for as you ascend to the C-suite.

Four Steps to Respond Effectively

Step 1: Don't rush. Timing can be the fine line between a reaction and a response. If you respond in haste, it may be from an emotional place and will be conveyed as a reaction. Clear and effective communication is nonemotional and based on evidence, not assumptions. When you take the time to carefully craft a response to an inquiry or request, the time allows you to set your personal feelings aside and focus on the result.

Whether it takes you an hour or one day to respond, think it through. Sometimes, a brief response takes the most time, so that you have the time to process the request. Use the time to redact all emotional language and ensure your response highlights your professional candor.

Step 2: Remain germane. Reactive communicators can get off-topic to make the other party feel the impact of their emotion. If the inquiry is about today's sales report, avoid reacting with a historical overview of what you've done for the company over the past five years. Only discuss the sales report.

Decision makers and gatekeepers are always seeking direct answers, not an overview of performance or dedication. Those issues will be covered another time. Besides, some of your emotional triggers may surface and turn the conversation from a response to a reaction.

Step 3: Avoid passiveness. As I highlighted in my conversation with a fellow writer on Facebook, I was direct in my responses. Instead of apologizing, minimizing, or allowing his deflection to impact my tone, while he was discussing politics, I responded to his reaction with a direct tone about the purpose of the interview, which is why I believe he changed his tone.

Never fight a reaction with a reaction, or you will go off-topic and lose control of your ability to lead the conversation. A reactive tone is passive because it is emotional and often done in haste. A response is purposeful and well crafted.

Step 4: Learn to use silence. Silence can also be the best response, or the only response needed. Silence can have several different interpretations within the communication spectrum. On one hand, it can imply that you don't care. On the other hand, it can also imply that whatever you're faced with is not worth a reply. No matter how you choose to use silence, this is a powerful gift, though only a select few use it well, as the next section explains.

Play Chess: The Gift of Silence

It takes a specific level of maturity to avoid falling into the reaction trap. Sometimes I think that people intentionally want to make you upset and see how combative you can be, instead of diffusing the tension. The workplace happens to be one of those places where there may be a heightened sense of tension and a competitive bitterness that is hard to break free from, especially when you have no idea who you are competing against. Getting to the top, or at least getting an invitation for an available seat at the table, has always felt like a complex game of checkers. How many people can be removed from the board to make your way to the top? I know you are reading this and thinking about the level of stress that you feel every day, and I have been through that walk and understand the pressure very well. But experience has taught me that the game of leadership is about letting competitive people play checkers, while collaborative people play chess, silently.

I reference chess many times because it is a game of pure strategy. The game is also about mastering the timing of the moves that will help you get as close to checkmate as possible. It is also designed for those who are willing to be patient, while thinking through their next move. Strategy is the only way to win a chess game, as your opponent cannot predict your next move. The goal of an effective chess game is to remain still as long as possible while thinking through every scenario that could impact your side of the board instead of moving in haste. It is the same strategy that will guide your communication style moving toward the C-suite.

When people know they cannot get a reaction out of you, they leave you alone. They know that you are a force of strength and very few things can impact your determination. It has been the winning strategy of my life, and I also believe that is why so many people are shocked by the successful transition I had from the corporate world to the business world. What they don't know is that I was silent but strategic. I never announced what I was working on, the partnerships I was brokering, the opportunities I was seeking, or the relationships that I had access to. While many people had so many negative things to say about what they thought I was doing, I was working in silence. I allowed people to say negative things, but I always understood that negative people are competitive, and I wanted to collaborate my way into bigger spaces.

Every inquiry, request, or correspondence does not deserve a reaction or a response. You need to learn when something requires your silence. It's our nature to announce our presence and our feelings, but you are strong enough to remain silent through it all. It does not mean that you are not affected; it just means that you know the value of your time. It's a liberating feeling when you can go from being a reactive person, to a responsive person, to silence.

The more you flex your silent muscle, the more you will attract the attention of leaders who understand and recognize the chess moves you are making, and that your choice to be silent is strategic. They know that you want to get to the C-suite because they understand that you are not playing checkers. You are not involving yourself in the office politics and the nonsense chatter of the day; you are completely invested and lending your voice to productive conversations that increase your value.

It is the same concept in business. I don't react to everything; there are some things I just leave my name out of. I can't tell you how many times a day some of my colleagues tag me on Twitter in different posts that they want my reaction to, and I just leave it there. They will barrage my phone with nonsense text messages asking me to check my Twitter page and get in a conversation, and I don't respond to the text nor the post. I have specific things to do, and I know that there are gatekeepers and decision makers paying attention to my every move, and sometimes the best thing I can do is not get involved in conversations that are not going to increase my wealth or my worth.

When you get to this level of becoming aware that you are being watched, and that every action (or inaction) has value, you will be strategic about your next move.

- Every post does not require your comment.
- Every email does not call for a reply.
- Every negative comment in the office does not need a response.

Some things require silence; and knowing when to lean on silence shows a level of growth. Eventually, you will go from silent to unaffected, and therefore focused and purposeful—and that's when the great opportunities will arise and you will have the energy to capitalize on them.

Cost-Benefit Analysis: A Professional Response in Business Decisions

Passive communication is rooted in our reactionary ways. While most of our reactions and responses are elicited by interpersonal dealings, there are situations that arise in careers that require we learn to respond versus react. Let's say your boss makes an unexpected request.

When we just snap out the words without thinking about whether agreeing to something benefits us in any way, we reveal our passive and reactionary ways. We want instead to prove we are powerful and professional in our responses by taking a pause to consider and analyze what is presented to us. The technical term for taking a pause to reflect, consider, and make a projection is "cost-benefit analysis," and I am quite keen on teaching this skill to women.

Before beginning any level of an excuse or lie to explain my own decisions, I think about whether the cost of saying yes outweighs the benefit of completing the task. I recently read about the cost-benefit analysis in Curtis Jackson's book, *Hustle Harder, Hustle Smarter.* Jackson, aka 50 Cent, is a well-known hip-hop artist who rose to fame in the early 2000s. However, he's quickly become a mogul in the world of film and television with several hit dramas on ABC and Starz Network. However, one of his most impressive public successes is his investment in Vitamin Water, which was acquired by Coca-Cola for an undisclosed figure. Don't let the rhetoric on Instagram fool you—50 Cent is a smart and intentional thinker, but until I read his book, I didn't realize that he also takes his time when making high-stake decisions and uses the cost-benefit analysis to avoid making decisions in haste, considering all aspects of his time before entering any partnership. He does not lend his name lightly.

As I hung onto every word, I thought about how many times we have been convinced to make decisions fast, and then, in the end, discover those rash judgments were the wrong ones. The name of the game if you want to be successful is to buy as much time as possible to make the best decisions for you. This is the difference between a reaction and a response. When I am approached with a media or interview opportunity, I always say I need a day to think about it. I must consider the future value of lending my name or my time to anything. I have spent many years saying yes and being passive, which mostly led to a dead-end road. I have countless stories about people who have screwed me out of lucrative deals and partnership opportunities, memberships, and so much more, all because I made passive and hasty decisions. Language is an intentional tool, one that when used correctly will set boundaries, manage expectations, and articulate when someone infringes on my goals. Relinquishing the habit of passive communication takes practice, but it also requires that we learn to avoid the most insidious of the passive traps: the habit of apologizing, which I cover in the next chapter.

7

Sorry for What?

Avoiding the Passive Apology

——— KEY TAKEAWAY ———

When you apologize for walking into a room or for speaking up in a meeting, you are communicating your fears and insecurities in front of others—especially to decision makers. As a consequence, this consistent level of apologetic communication has extended the journey of women to close the gap in the C-suite.

One snowy January evening in New York City, way before cell phones, the last train home was delayed due to the inclement weather. I panicked. I stayed at the office to keep calling the railroad. Every two minutes or so, I called to ensure that the train was still coming. Otherwise, I was going to have to call a friend to brave the snow and pick me up, or find a friend whose couch I could crash on until the next day. I didn't want to explore either of these options, but the reality was that the snow was mounting fast.

One of the founding partners, who had never uttered a word to me in the year that I had been a receptionist at his firm, came off of the elevator and said, "What are you still doing here? Do you know how bad it is out there?" In my mind, I wanted to ask him for the keys to his new Range Rover so I could go home, but I decided to keep my humor to myself and smile. In my high-pitched "nice girl" voice, I said, "I'm just sitting here to wait for an update on the railroad to get back to Brooklyn."

He responded, "Oh, Brooklyn! That's a distance. You might want to find another way in case the train does not come tonight." As I took a deep breath and thought about his statement, I responded, "I have a few alternative plans if I'm unable to get back to Brooklyn. Do you mind if I hang out here until the railroad is updated?"

"No problem at all," he said.

About an hour later, the train arrived, and I proceeded to the station. I didn't even have a moment to say goodbye to those who were still in the office, but that was not uncommon as many of the founding attorneys and partners had limited interaction with the support staff, or administrative staff for that matter. My departure without announcement was part of the office culture. But I should've known that having a brief conversation about my personal experience with the partner, who had never spoken to me before, never even returned a "good morning" had an ulterior motive.

The next day, although the snow had stopped, the train was once again delayed due to the previous day's inclement weather. It felt like a scene out of *Groundhog Day*. At 7 p.m., I dialed the railroad station to find out what time the train was coming. The same partner walked out of the elevator and passed the reception area, and he said the same thing again: "What are you still doing here?" I repeated the same answer from the day before: "I'm just waiting for the train."

"Since you're going to be here for a minute," he said, "can you go get a few bagels, about 10 sandwiches, coffee, and a few slices of cake from the deli downstairs and set it up in the conference room? Let them bill it to the firm, and set up the conference room for 10 people. Thanks."

I thought to myself, *This is not my job description, but maybe I should just do it for now, and maybe he might take notice of my initiative and think of me when it is time to consider staff assignments or promotions.* I responded, "Sure."

I went downstairs to the deli, brought the order back into the conference room as requested, and set up the room for 10 people. I'd heard stories about these after-work conferences that happened with the partners and potential clients. After I set up the room, I called the train station again to make sure I didn't miss my train—I had about 30 minutes until the train arrived at the station. I put on my coat and left to catch my train.

The next morning, I walked into the office and this same partner came out into the reception area and said, "Where did you go last night? I had other things that I needed to be done before you left. You could have at least told me you were leaving."

"I'm so sorry, but my train was on the way and I had to go," I replied. I started a long chain of explanations and apologies to ease the tension. Even while I was apologizing, I debated why I was apologizing and explaining myself when I had done him a courtesy.

Why was I explaining myself to someone who did not value the relationship of his administrative staff until he needed a favor after hours and I just happened to be in the building? Why was I apologizing for catching the last train back to New York City during a blizzard? I had done the work, acting in the catering capacity beyond the scope of the agreement I had with the firm, so why was I apologizing for going home? Why was I apologizing in public with a smile on my face in a manner that was pleasing to someone who was disrespecting me?

The answer was simple: I have listened to women apologizing all of my life. How many times have you unintentionally apologized in public?

"Sorry" as you walk in the door to a meeting where your presence was expected.

"Sorry for running late" for being one minute late to the office.

"Sorry to bother you" for asking your HR manager for a promotion or raise.

"Sorry, I disagree" when making an important point during a board meeting.

"Sorry" for the need to leave early for personal reasons.

We've all done it; you're not alone. As a self-proclaimed recovering sorry-o-holic, I understand the pressure of trying to balance other people's expectations, while also balancing real life. The closer I moved to the C-suite, the more I had to be aware of what I was apologizing for. Although innocent in meaning, the unintended consequence of consistently apologizing is and continues to remain that it is a self-limiting form of communication.

You've probably unintentionally said "sorry" because:

- You don't feel equally qualified
- You are concerned about people-pleasing
- You are weak
- You're too emotional
- You are an over-explainer

More importantly, apologizing is impulsive. I have read numerous studies that call this form of apology "hedging"—a way to measure the temperature in the room or to build a rapport with others before joining a conversation. Although that is quite fascinating, men simply don't hedge in an introduction—they just jump right in and start talking.

For example, at the start of the Covid-19 pandemic, I worked in my home office most of the day during the quarantine. If my son had a question, he would walk into my office and say, "excuse me," then ask his question. On the other hand, my niece who spent some time with me at the beginning of quarantine walked to my office and immediately said, "I'm sorry to bother you, Auntie," to which I would respond, "That's okay, talk to me." My son does not feel the need to apologize for interrupting me, but my niece is expected to apologize. Introductory apologies like this are impulsive and a common mannerism, which is the result of hetero-normative conditioning and expectations. It is imperative to remind yourself that an apology will not come off as a confident introduction in the presence of decision-makers. Replace "I'm sorry" with "excuse me" and stop apologizing.

It's a Scientific Fact

Karina Schumann, social program chair of psychology at the University of Pittsburgh and coauthor of "Why Women

Apologize More Than Men: Gender Differences in Thresholds for Perceiving Offensive Behavior," conducted a study of 33 women, ages 18 to 44, to identify how women unintentionally apologize unjustly. In her findings, as paraphrased by *Live Science*, "it's not that men are reluctant to admit wrongdoing, the study shows. It's just that they have a higher threshold for what they think warrants reparation. . . . Women might have a lower threshold for what requires an apology because they are more concerned with the emotional experiences of others and with promoting harmony in their relationships."

Apologetic and limiting language is an unintentional and learned behavior, which is often viewed as a level of respect or invoking common mannerisms, such as saying "good morning" when you enter your office in the morning, or "see you tomorrow" when you are leaving. Although apologizing for the simplest things that you do that inflict pain or impact the lives of others is completely acceptable, when you apologize for walking into a room or for speaking up in a meeting, you are communicating your fears and insecurities in front of others—especially to decision makers. As a consequence, I believe this consistent level of apologetic communication has extended the journey of women to close the gap in the C-suite. Unapologetic leaders are not looking for the next apologetic leader to sit at the table. Besides, what are you apologizing for?

Unintentionally, women express apologetic behaviors beyond verbal communication into written communication. On an average day, I receive over 100 emails from women who have at least two apologies within a simple five-line email, and I am often confused about what the apology is for.

I once read an email from someone who wrote, "I'm sorry to email you this late, but . . ." The same email ended with, "once again I'm so sorry to email you this late and please accept my apology."

In 2018, Tami Reiss, Steve Brudz, Manish Kakwani, and Eric Tillberg developed the plug-in for Gmail called the Just Not Sorry app. The purpose of the plugin is to highlight the number of times you have apologized in an email before you send it. According to a Monica Torres op-ed and review published by TheLadders.com entitled, "This Chrome email plugin wants you to stop saying 'sorry' all the time," the plugin seeks to "stop qualifying your message and diminishing your voice by pointing out your use of 'sorry' in emails, so that we edit ourselves from using them."

The Just Not Sorry app is a constant reminder in all red about how you use minimizing language and minimizing tones with an apologetic theme throughout your correspondence as you are writing it. It is done in real time to allow you to see how you unintentionally communicate via email. I think it's a genius move considering the level of accountability that is needed to remind you to amplify your voice. When you apologize consistently, especially in a simple correspondence, you highlight your insecurities. Never begin a correspondence with "I'm sorry" or "Let me apologize before we get started"—this is essentially saying, "I know I don't deserve to be here," or "I'm not qualified to be here, but. . . ."

There is one specific notable reason why women apologize repeatedly—modesty. According to IGI Global in its *Encyclopedia of Strategic Leadership and Management*, feminine modesty is "Women's tendency to under-represent their achievements; whereas men promote their accomplishments."

We are conditioned as young girls to "cover up" and smile with a shy demeanor as a way to hinder young women from celebrating their accomplishments. We are taught to be modest and less boastful in the presence of others. Hence, we believe that it can be perceived as "impolite" to brag or to accept public praise for our exceptional work. Instead, we spread the praise among a team, rather than own our qualifications as leaders.

Naomi Osaka defeated 23X Grand Slam winner Serena Williams to win the 2018 U.S. Open, becoming Japan's first-ever tennis player to win a Grand Slam tournament. When Naomi accepted the trophy during her victory speech, she said "I'm so sorry it had to end like this." Serena came over and embraced her to show Naomi that she should accept her win as an accomplishment and to stop apologizing for her victory. Naomi later stated on NBC's Today show, "I just felt very emotional, and I felt that I had to apologize." It was a statement that left many tennis fans confused. An editorial by Nastaran Tavakoli-Far in *The Lily*, entitled "Naomi Osaka apologizing for winning is the other tragedy of the U.S. Open," stated "the feeling that she had to somehow apologize for her brilliance and downplay her achievements is a quandary women still grapple with. Now, let's also start talking about why women have to apologize and worry about everyone's feelings when they've done nothing wrong, and especially when they've shown their greatness and strength in the process."

Modesty is also an inherited behavior that starts with young girls. I have spent most of my adult years unlearning my upbringing to detach myself from this level of modesty. As a child, I would strive for academic excellence in school, only to go home with excitement as I shared my great news with joy, to listen to my grandmother react by saying, "I'm very proud of you, but don't show off in front of your cousins. Find a way to encourage them, not discourage them." I thought to myself, *Huh? I did all of this work and I can't share it?* Meanwhile, when my older male cousins passed their driver's test, there was an entire celebration to acknowledge their milestones.

Female modesty is also conditioned by other women in the workplace. More notable than how women unintentionally downplay their achievements at work by communicating a level of deflection to avoid public praise, there is also an element of women versus women that contributes to this level of public modesty. Let's have an honest discussion—women do not like to be labeled as a "bitch" or "difficult to work with," which is a common level of judgment from other women. We subconsciously encourage women to be "liked" more than respected, so high-achieving women will revert to feminine modesty to avoid hindering relationships at work and limit any element of favoritism.

A 2017 editorial in *The Atlantic*, called *Why Do Women Bully Each Other at Work?* references a blog titled *Beware the Female Biglaw Partner* by Shannon Forchheimer. Forchheimer, an attorney who practices in Washington, DC, outlines a simple argument about why women do not support each other in the workplace. She identifies three types of women in the workplace:

"aggressive bitch"

"passive-aggressive bitch,"

"tuned-out, indifferent bitch"

In almost every study I have read over the past decade, the overall thesis for why women universally apologize comes from an emotional state of wanting to be accepted, not judged, and to avoid future conflicts. I also believe that women simply want to be liked, and by using an apologetic mannerism, they will come across as engaging and sweet, rather than qualified or being perceived as too masculine. By diminishing our voices, we start every thought with a public apology.

I gave a talk at a university for a charity organization within the school recently, and the microphone was a headset two-piece with a microphone box on the back. I was wearing a taffeta dress that I happen to love, and if you know anything about me, the first thing you will see is my well-done short pixie cut hair that I have spent years caring for. I have been obsessed with my hair since I was 12 years old when I was allowed to have my first professional haircut. Since that moment, my genuine affection for my hair began and has never swayed. When I walked up to the podium to start my talk and saw this headpiece, as a hair connoisseur, I refused to put anything on top of my hair or a mic box on the back of my very expensive A-line taffeta dress. With an audience of onlookers, I decided to wrap the headpiece of the microphone around my neck so that I could have full animation from the stage while holding the microphone box. It was a last-minute move because I was not aware that this institution did not have handheld microphones or a lectern. I did not think about it as a laborious task until the speech was over.

Hundreds of women walked up to me after the event, and although I expected them to give me feedback about my talk or to ask questions on how they could negotiate in the workplace, I received hundreds of questions about how I found the confidence to not apologize for not wearing the headpiece. It was something that I had never thought about. I was more concerned about my hair and less concerned about the appearance of the headset around my neck. While others would compromise and begin the apology of saying, "I'm sorry, I cannot wear this headpiece," I decided to work my way and make it work for me. I was in shock about how people were utterly surprised by my decision not to apologize for a technical snafu, but I could not have prepared to walk into an institution that did not have a handheld lavalier microphone. Either way, I did not owe anyone an explanation or an apology for making the decision not to put anything on my hair that would obstruct the beautiful curls that I worked so hard to maintain.

How to Stop Apologizing: Emotional Freedom Technique (EFT)

To avoid the impulse to apologize, you have to be aware that it is happening. An impulsive decision is like purchasing gum at the checkout counter of the supermarket—it's just there, so you pick it up, pay, and go. It's not a purchase that requires lots of thought, reading the ingredients, or asking any questions. Our communicative impulses are triggered by fear and our connection with feminine modesty. Ironically, many of us are unaware that we apologize, but we are very aware of the triggers that cause some of our passive behaviors, and there is a way to work on unlearning the habit.

One of the most effective techniques that I have found over the years to help me control the impulse of apologizing is the EFT—Emotional Freedom Techniques, also referred to as tapping. I learned about this method many years ago when I was struggling with my wealth consciousness around asking for money. There was a time in my life when I first started my business when the moment someone would ask me how much I charge, I would frequently and impulsively discount my value because my wealth consciousness was at a low frequency. I would scatter around the conversation to imply that I would work for free when I knew that the survival of my company depended on generating consistent profit, especially when I had staff that depended on their paycheck each week. I was invited to an EFT session, and I thought that this was completely off the rails and far beyond the scope of anything I would ever want to do, but I was wrong. Today, I find myself tapping at the moment that my frequency runs low to remind myself that I am worthy of everything that I ask for and nothing but abundance surrounds me.

I am not an EFT expert or life coach, but as a believer, I've seen the benefits of tapping frequently in moments of anxiety. According to the principles of EFT, there are points on the body that contain meridian points and vibrations, which similar to the practice of acupuncture, it is believed that vital energy flows through these points. By using two of your fingers to tap meridian points on the top of your head, the center of your forehead, underneath your eyes, underneath your nose, underneath your lips, near your collarbone, on the palm of your hand, and underneath your eyes, you tap into these meridian points as you are stating out loud what you believe you deserve. Healers such as Pamela Bruner and Iyanla Vanzant have all used EFT in their healing rituals when working with high-power celebrities to overcome past traumas in their life.

The moment I feel myself at a low energy frequency when I'm about to discuss money, I tap my forehead. It starts to raise my frequency level when I put my hand in the motion to get close to my head. It removes the element of anxiety without the need to feel overwhelmed by making a decision. Although I know you are here to find out ways to communicate more effectively, if you don't overcome your anxiety, the moment you are at your lowest frequency, you will enter the room and apologize. By using this technique before your next meeting, or even on your way to your office, you are changing the frequency and reminding yourself that there's nothing to apologize for, and setting the intention to avoid any impulsive statement that might critically harm your career.

Tapping your meridian points will change your energy frequency. The need to make an impulse apology never truly goes away, but the tapping will remind you to change your verbiage. With EFT, I always believe you have to have an assignment for tapping, so when you set the intention around tapping, you start with explaining the intention before you start.

- I will not apologize today.
- I will not say "I'm sorry" in a meeting.
- I have nothing to apologize for.
- I belong.
- I deserve a seat at the table.
- I'm a leader.

If you start by saying these statements in combination with tapping, you use the affirmations to connect with the intention of why you are tapping. It is just the energy from your comfort zone to connect you with the thing you were most fearful of doing. I will admit, even with tapping you might slip a few times and apologize, but with consistency in repetition, with time it will end.

Apologizing is a difficult habit to break, so be patient with yourself. We are so hard on ourselves that we rarely celebrate our one win of the day. Perhaps your one win is adding vegetables to your diet. The moment you commit to it, it's a win. Maybe you apologize eight times per day, but if you avoid the impulse to apologize at least once, then celebrate it. Now, you have seven more to go. Each milestone is worthy of acknowledgment and a step in the right direction.

The most effective way to replace apologizing in your professional vocabulary is to remind yourself to use gratitude. I had the pleasure of meeting Maja Jovanovic at a talk on confidence at Harvard Business School in 2020. In her TED Talk, "How Apologies Kill Our Confidence," Maja said, "If you are beginning and ending your sentences with 'Sorry,' people aren't looking at you going *Damn! How can I get some of that confidence!* Or *hey, how can I promote that woman?* Anything other than 'Thank you' when praised makes you sound doubtful of your accomplishments [and] self-worth."

Whenever I feel the impulse driving me toward entering a room and saying "I'm sorry," I begin a tapping routine on the side of my hand, and begin a silent affirmation by repeating "Thank you." By using terms of gratitude, you will shift the impulse and create a new habit loop.

In his bestselling book, *The Power of Habit*, Charles Duhigg discusses the elements of a habit loop. I was introduced to Duhigg's work by a friend who was working on identifying the cause of his inability to onboard new clients for his marketing firm. His biggest fear was rejection, so he was undercharged to avoid the uncomfortable money discussion around value. My friend discussed how he found that his fear of money was a "cue from my mother," because he grew up extremely poor, while his mother believed in a life of servitude, by teaching her son to give more than he received. The breakthroughs that my friend was experiencing were life-changing; I had to read them myself.

Duhigg clearly describes how his "3 p.m. cookie habit" caused him to search for the cause of his daily sweet treat routine. He says that the more something becomes a habit, the less you have to think. According to the article in ScienceDaily titled "How we form habits, change existing ones." by Wendy Wood, provost professor of psychology and business at the University of Southern California, "Studies show that about 40 percent of people's daily activities are performed each day in almost the same situations. . . . When the habitual mind is engaged, our habits function largely outside of awareness."

Essentially, the habit of apologizing, coupled with our inherited behavior of modesty, is nothing more than just a sound bite in our mind that is playing on a loop. Unfortunately, because the loop is playing all day, you may not even realize how many times you have apologized today. It's on automatic replay.

The habit loop as described by Duhigg consists of three parts: A routine, a reward, and a cue.

The following steps and examples will help you to start breaking any habit.

The Routine

Let's say you have a weekly sales meeting with 20 managers and stakeholders to discuss benchmarks for your team. While everyone is speaking up and often over each other, you have a few strategies of your own you believe are necessary to direct the conversation. You feel the impulse to say, "I'm sorry, excuse me . . ." as you have done at previous meetings to request a moment to speak.

This is the moment to identify the routine and all of the triggers that create this loop. In this example, the meetings are held weekly in a free-flowing manner. You may not have noticed that you have apologized in every meeting around the same time as it is habitual. The loop in this scenario is the weekly meetings and the lack of structure. Now you know what causes you to apologize.

Experiment with Rewards

Test different hypotheses to determine what is driving your impulse to apologize. For example:

- Intimidation
- Feeling unprepared
- Being overwhelmed
- Don't want to come across as arrogant or rude
- You can't stand sitting through these meetings
- Feeling ignored
- Simply don't know why you apologize

Write down when you apologized and what you apologized for each week when you attend the meeting. After you identify when and why you can begin creating a new pattern or habit to replace your normal "I'm sorry" routine.

In the previous example where you feel the impulse to apologize, think about the tangible reward you have gained as a result of apologizing—everyone begins listening to you, or maybe your boss says, "That's a great point." The past reward has been that you believe your voice was heard, but maybe it was not valued.

Recognize the Cue

According to *The Power of Habit*, , the reason why it is so hard to identify the cues that trigger our habits is that "there is too much information bombarding us as our behaviors unfold. Experiments have shown that almost all habitual cues fit into one of five categories:

Location

Time

Emotional State

Other People

Immediately preceding action

The most important part of isolating the cue is to document each emotion regularly. When I was breaking up with my apologetic addiction, my turning point during this exercise was identifying the person in the office who made me feel invisible and undervalued. It was the breakthrough I needed to stop giving one person so much of my power and attention.

By isolating the cue, you are getting to the root of the habit. For you, it may be cultural, instinctive, or maybe someone at work that makes you feel intimidated—whatever it is, you must identify it. It is like pinpointing the reason why a car doesn't start—it must be diagnosed to find the root cause of the issue.

You will learn some very interesting truths about yourself when you decide to take a deeper dive into your unintentional behaviors. In my previous professional interactions, I realized that my cue was a specific person. Once I identified the cue and thought about my routine, I experimented with a new type of reward, which helped me to stop apologizing in a room filled with hundreds of people because I was affected by one person.

The Great Gratitude Response

Unless you unintentionally knock someone out when opening a door or hit someone over the head with a baseball bat while playing with your kids in the park, save your sorry! You will need it for the big things later in life. For now, keep in mind that apologizing has the same effect as discounting your value or dimming your light. Let me give you a few alternatives to practice as you are growing your one-win mentality.

When you're walking into a meeting, instead of saying, "I'm sorry," rephrase it with gratitude:

Thanks for waiting on me, I appreciate it.

When you're about to speak to your HR manager about a raise, instead of saying "I'm sorry," rephrase it with gratitude:

I am looking forward to having this discussion with you. Thank you for carving out some time in your day to meet with me.

If there is a meet up after optional work, but you have something personal to attend to, instead of saying "I'm sorry I can't be there," rephrase it with gratitude:

Thank you for thinking of me, but I have other personal obligations today.

If there is an opportunity to volunteer at work, and after analyzing the cost-benefit, you have decided that it is not worth your time, rather than saying "I'm sorry," rephrase it:

Thank you for offering me the opportunity, but I do not think it is a match for me at this time.

If you were in a meeting when people were speaking over each other, it is not a time to say I'm sorry or excuse me. If you have a point that you believe is relevant to the discussion, rephrase your interjection with gratitude:

I have a few points that I believe are relevant to this meeting and to guide our discussion, and I would appreciate it if I can add value to our conversation today.

Let's say there's a project at work that you believe would be an excellent opportunity to be considered for a promotion or significant increase in compensation. Instead of walking up to the decision maker and saying, "I'm sorry, but can I talk to you? I promise it will only take a minute," rephrase it with gratitude:

I recently learned about the new opportunity to work on the Wall Street project, and I would like to be considered in the vetting process for prospective team members. I believe I could be a tremendous asset to this opportunity and welcome a discussion to reassess my qualifications with you when you have a moment. Thank you.

If you are sending an email to a customer, client, associate, investor, or partner, never start the first sentence with an apology. Instead rephrase it with gratitude:

I was unable to reply to your email earlier due to unforeseen circumstances. However, I'm working diligently to fix the problem and should have an answer for you no later than 5 p.m. today. If you have any questions, never hesitate to contact me directly.

If you are at a public event and would like to ask a question, instead of starting the sentence with "I'm sorry," rephrase it with gratitude:

Thank you for selecting me. I have a question about _____

If someone decides to highlight a grammatical or spelling error that you have in a report (publicly or privately), instead of saying "I'm sorry," rephrase it with gratitude:

Thank you for bringing that to my attention. The revisions will be made shortly.

If someone responds negatively to your post or opinion on social media, instead of finding common ground through starting your response with "I'm sorry," rephrase it with gratitude:

I appreciate your opinion and thank you for sharing it.

If someone asks you to jump on the phone with her but you do not have the time, instead of apologizing, rephrase it with gratitude:

I appreciate your business. My schedule does not permit a quick call at the moment. Feel free to send me your questions by email or contact my assistant.

The most important factors to remember:

- Document yourself and beware of your apologetic language. Remind yourself that it takes time to break old patterns and habits.
- Try EFT to transition away from impulsive communication. Use specific navigational phrases to hold yourself accountable for the behavior.

- Watch out for habit loops and the cues that lead to making specific self-limiting communication decisions.
- Replace "sorry" with gratitude.

The common goal of eliminating the impulse of saying "I'm sorry" does not eliminate the habit of responding defensively. You must respond less apologetically by creating a sense of urgency around your EFT practices and remembering your cues to eliminate habitual loops that connect you to old communication patterns.

The only time you should say "I'm sorry" is when you have something to be sorry for. Again I want you to be patient with yourself during this transition. As a former apologetic woman, I'm constantly reminding myself to practice gratitude, but habits take a lifetime to break, especially if they have been conditioned as part of the gender narrative of girls.

8

The Power and Precision of Prepositions
Learning the Little Words That Go a Long Way

KEY TAKEAWAY

Mastering middle school English grammar can make the difference between a passive reaction and a powerful response.

One of my childhood memories is from eighth grade with my English teacher, Dr. Kumar, at the Montessori School of New York, as she drilled us daily about the list of complex and non complex prepositional phrases. She would say, "Anything after the preposition is an option. It's not necessary to complete the sentence." I used to think this woman was crazy and that I would never need to know any of these grammar rules to be successful in life. I was so wrong and so naive to think that the ability to articulate would not be a necessary element in climbing the corporate ladder. I wish

I could find Dr. Kumar and apologize for underestimating an entire semester of prepositions and prepositional phrases. Today, this rule helps me masterfully communicate not only in my professional life but when speaking on stage.

If you can't articulate it, you can't get it. The law of prepositions is the key to breaking the habit of explaining oneself, so you can get what you want and deserve by clearly communicating your value. Think of it this way: Prepositions break a sentence into two parts—the decision and the explanation. When used with a passive voice, prepositional phrases will impede your success. When used powerfully, they will help you create value-adding conversations with key decision makers at work.

The Passive Prepositional Phrase

The preposition *because* is my trigger word. It splits the decision from the explanation, and the moment I hear it, I do my best to hold both myself and others accountable to avoid any further details. As we discussed in the habit loop for "I'm sorry" in Chapter 7, make sure you document when you say the word "because" as much as possible. Also, remain cautious and mindful of those who ask you "why" or "why not," as those people provide clues to what triggers you to start using a passive voice and prepositions.

Similar to how interjection words such as *and* and *but* can connect two parts of a sentence that are either related or unrelated, a preposition can trap you into connecting a decision to an excuse. Although the intention is innocent, everything after the preposition is unnecessary to the context of the thought. As Dr. Kumar said, it's optional. In both written and oral communication, prepositions are unnecessary, and anything that follows a preposition can be deemed as an afterthought, hence, no explanation is required. It is the part of the sentence the receiver, most especially in business, does not care about (more on this in the next chapter, "The 8-Minute Rule").

Anytime you use words or phrases such as . . .

- Because
- As long as
- Until I
- I think so
- Except for

. . . you become susceptible to being talked into tasks you don't want to do or you know won't help your career (or out of something you do want to do). By using one of the above-mentioned prepositions, you are cornering yourself to continue the sentence with the excuse or explanation.

Let's say that your boss asks you to consider volunteering on a team project on Saturday, and you cannot make it because you promised to take your kids out for ice cream.

The No Explanation Required response is:
Unfortunately, I cannot come in this weekend.

The prepositional phrase response is:
Unfortunately, I cannot come in this weekend because I promised the kids to take them out for ice cream.

Your boss did not ask you what you were doing over the weekend, but to come to work voluntarily on Saturday. By disclosing details that are not a directive to your decision, you're offering additional information that could potentially be used to redirect your decision. You can still be polite and up front with a clear response without the need to continue your sentence with a preposition. However, because many women anticipate the next question (usually "why"), they use a preposition to offer the answer to a question that hasn't come yet. To avoid a "dreaded" follow-up question, we blanket the entire decision with all of the details to substantiate our thought process.

Complex Prepositions

I don't mean to turn this chapter into a middle school grammar class, but this is a clear way to understand how easily an explanation is created, and how easy it would be to stop.

Consider the prepositional phrase "because of" and the words after it in the following sentence:

We can't play tennis today [because of the rain.]

Here's the same example without the explanation:

We can't play tennis today.

This short statement is not rude or crass, nor is it unreasonable. It is direct and describes the action and intent without the need to justify your decision. When you reach this level of confidence, it is liberating and solidifies you as a qualified leader who provides directives, not excuses.

The same preposition, *because*, can create a poorly constructed, long-winded correspondence with additional facts that are not germane to the conversation. For example:

I'm so sorry I did not email you back yesterday because we had to leave early due to the inclement weather.

Neither the reference to the inclement weather nor the opening apology is necessary. Yet, we see it time and time again. Anything after the preposition *because* is not relevant to the conversation. In other words, stick to the facts and don't give any explanations.

On the other hand, prepositional phrases, if used correctly, can work in your favor, especially if you're seeking a promotion or advancement in your career. When you use a prepositional phrase to substantiate your value, it is the break between the ask and providing evidence. I refer to opportunity meetings or negotiation conversations as "Increase Your Ask," which is also the name of the negotiation arm of my company. I won't go into too much detail here, but we advise women that if they are going to use prepositions and prepositional phrases in their verbal and nonverbal communications, they should use it to increase their ask.

The "Increase-Your-Ask" Prepositional Phrase

When you're using prepositional phrases in an opportunity conversation, the decision or the ask coupled with the prepositional phrases should end with substantiating evidence to support the ask. This creates a cohesive thought process and evidence-based approach to value-add conversations at work. This approach to the prepositional phrase turns a passive discussion into a value-based conversation. Once you master using prepositions and prepositional phrases to create value for yourself, you'll avoid entering into passive discussions. Earn new opportunities *because* you have learned how to ask for something; switch the direction and justify your position within the ask. For example:

I want to discuss your consideration of a raise because I have increased the value of the sales department within this company by over 200 percent over the last three years as a team lead.

The beginning of the structure of the sentence starts with the ask, then it is broken up by the word *because* to set up the transition, and then it ends with substantiating evidence to support the ask. By using a preposition in this way, you are having a productive conversation. However, in my daily conversations with women around negotiating, I found they turn a strong ask into a passive conversation due to fear of sounding "assertive" or "greedy." For example:

I want to discuss your consideration of a raise because I really love what I do and I think I'm good at it.

This is the passive approach. Leaving both an explanation and substantiating proof off the table turns your ask into a passive conversation. Similar to the reactive communicator, which we discussed in Chapter 6, this passive approach of softening your ask could be triggered by the fear of rejection. This is why women often miss the mark on negotiating— they set out with one intention and talk themselves out of it, most commonly by thinking, *What if they say no?* The preposition is to be used as a turning point in the conversation, in fact, in all conversations. However, the preposition can become the turning point that triggers fear. In my interactions with some of my clients in The Confidence Factor for Women, they have indicated that the transition point of the preposition in a conversation or correspondence, especially if they are about to discuss compensation, increases their anxiety. Using your prepositions in a responsive way, however, changes the intention of the conversation. When you read "The 8-Minute Rule" in the next chapter, you will learn how to create micro conversations that will help you to set the intention and get to the point faster. Sometimes, the anxiety is a sign that you are not focused on the outcome; hence, you become nervous and begin explaining.

Thanks to Dr. Kumar, I never forget any of my prepositions, and they have served as cues to remember that anything said or written after the preposition *must* create value. Otherwise, don't use one.

The preposition is a life hack to hold yourself accountable to the transition points in simple conversations. I have provided a list of useful prepositions and prepositional phrases; study them well and take note of when you use them and in what direction you want the conversation to go. One trick that works best for me is to slow down and listen to myself as I'm using a preposition, then discern if I'm going in the direction of value or getting ready to highlight my vulnerabilities. It's also a great way to keep specific conversations short and sweet. Remember, anything after the preposition is not necessary unless it's a value-add conversation.

If we learn to not react on the basis of doing what we think people want us to do so they like us, and pause to do a cost-benefit analysis (discussed in Chapter 6), we will create habits of thoughtful response that include avoiding passive prepositions and knowing when to use powerful ones. So, there's no need to explain why you cannot make it to happy hour this afternoon with your coworkers, "no" or "no thanks" are full sentences. We discussed gratitude as a communication tool, and you can easily respond by saying, "Thank you for inviting me, but I will not be able to make happy hour today." There is gratitude, a clear directive, a clear decision, and no explanation. Do you see how simple that is?

Be aware of your voice, your words, and your reactions versus responses. There is a difference between decision-based responses and meaningless jargon. If the reasoning is essential to the decision, there may be an exception. Otherwise, keep in mind that anything you say after the preposition *because* is not needed. You have already stated your decision. That is how high-performance leaders separate themselves from average ones.

9

The 8-Minute Rule

Mastering the Art of Micro Conversations

When I was in my twenties and navigating my way in a dog-eat-dog legal profession, I was rear-ended on the Southern State Parkway on my way to work. No one was hurt, but my car was damaged significantly. Adrenaline flooding my veins, instead of calling the police, I called my office manager.

Hi, Kathy! I was just in a major car accident on the Southern State around Exit 19. This guy came out of nowhere and just slammed into the back of my car. My neck jolted and I didn't know where I was for just a second—potentially I have a concussion, but I don't know yet. I'm waiting for the police to arrive, hopefully, I will find out if I'm going to make it. This guy just came out of nowhere, and every day when I turn this corner I pray that no one ever slams into the back of my car, but today it happened."

I nearly lost my breath rattling on with my explanations to Kathy. In retrospect, I wanted some sympathy and a bit of attention. Instead, Kathy gave me exactly what I needed when she responded, "So are you going to come to work or not?"

Whoa. She's heartless, I thought. But I know now, 20 years later, that Kathy was right.

There are only two answers that matter—yes or no. Kathy gave me a dose of reality, and wanted a short answer to the only important questions: "Are you on your way to work, or do you need a day off?"

Welcome to the world of working for lawyers. But her response was one that I needed to hear: *Get to the point.* It was a harsh lesson that I needed to learn as early as possible if I wanted to climb the corporate ladder and earn a seat at the table. Even further, no one is listening. You may believe that people who react to your explanations care, until you realize they only care about the answer or decision that affects them. They don't care about the explanation that led you to the decision. The drawn-out monologues to our decision are often more tedious to the person listening than they are to us. You believe they care, but here's some straight talk: no one gives a crap about your personal life.

Drop the Neurotic Narrative

Implementing the KISS principle (Keep It Short and Simple) is the best way to accelerate to the C-suite. Many books, famed lectures, and TED Talks discuss effective communication and the importance of mindfulness and empathy one must possess. However, women rarely fit into this broad category. We communicate from a different narrative than men. We subscribe to an internal memo that expects us to be quiet, yet apologetic with an elongated narrative to substantiate our own decisions and intentions. Overexplaining is a form of apologizing. We overexplain everything while undervaluing our contributions as leaders. What happens when we offer unnecessary elaborations to our final decisions is that we show our leaks; we open ourselves up to be persuaded otherwise, and that sends a signal that we are not leaders at all. Decisions should be well thought out, confident, and final, which shows a team your word matters. Watch Mary sabotage herself in the following scenario by revealing the weakness in her decision.

The choice to go to the movie and for drinks is completely optional, but most of the people at the company are going. The manager walks up to Mark and says, "Mark, we are all going to the movies and happy hour at a local pub today after work at five. Do you want to go?"

Mark responds, "No thanks. Have a great weekend." He nonchalantly clicks his alarm off on his Tesla and drives off for a weekend of fun by himself.

Mary, on the other hand, is gathering her things and shutting down the computer for the weekend. "Hey, Mary," the manager says. "We're all going to the movies and the pub after work today for some drinks. Do you want to join us?"

Mary is known for being a team player, and she's always thinking about what's best for the team rather than herself. *It was a great win,* she thinks, *I feel bad now that I would prefer to go home than spend more time at work but not at work.*

Mary's response:

> *Aw man . . . sheesh, I wish I knew sooner. I want to come out with you guys tonight, but I bought a chuck roast and rosemary to put in my slow cooker tonight from a recipe that I want to try that I saw Bobby Flay make on the Food Network. The recipe says I need eight hours to get it all ready for tomorrow. I want to come, but I want to cook this chuck roast, too. Let me see what I can do. Maybe I can go home right now to prepare it and try to see if I can meet you back at the movie theater at seven or even later for drinks at the pub.*

They don't call it TMI for nothing, okay? Mary's elongated explanation provides too many unclear personal details about her decision. Essentially, Mary is saying that she wants to cook the chuck roast, which is nobody's business. This is an optional after-work event, but the explanation she provides leaves more facts about her personal life than about her decision. It leaves her susceptible for an effective manager to litigate her decision by giving her options on how to prepare the chuck roast and still be at the movie theater on time.

No one needs to know why you said no. When Mark said, "no thanks," and drove off in the Tesla, no one asked him why or asked him to explain himself. There is an expectation that men make decisions while women will make revisions. I have never heard anyone ask a man to explain his no. If Mary just said no, the next common question that could have opened up the floodgates of explaining herself would be "Why?" It is uncommon for men to be asked why.

Mary's waffled response is common. Women are conditioned to be nice to everyone, which includes smiling when we don't feel like it, saying hello to people we do not care for, and working in strenuous environments that take a toll on our health just to please others. We convince ourselves that the narrative matters more than the answer, so we respond with a decision and then explain that decision in long form. We feel guilty about our decision on either side of the scale. Hence, in the books written about effective communication and how to communicate with compassion, women do not see or hear themselves throughout the pages, because it does not reflect the way women communicate in the workplace.

To test my example, we surveyed 100 women about leadership and professional boundaries. The question on the survey asked, "If a colleague, coworker, client, or partner asked you to stay late to work on a project (it's an optional assignment) that you cannot attend because you have a previous personal engagement or commitment, how would you respond?" Sixty-six of our respondents chose the option that offers too many personal details.

What Not to Do

The following examples show what to do and what not to do when communicating a decision.

> **Do:** *I'm running 20 minutes late for our scheduled meeting.*

> **Don't:** *I'm running 20 minutes late to our scheduled meeting because my son's school called, and I had to turn back in the middle of traffic. I'm so sorry.*

Do: *I want to discuss an opportunity to contribute to the sales development department as a team leader.*

Don't: *I want to discuss the opportunity to contribute to the sales development department as a team leader because I believe I have been here the longest, and I know the ins and outs of this company.*

Do: *I would like to set up a meeting to discuss a potential joint venture.*

Don't: *I would like to set up a meeting to discuss a potential joint venture between our companies because I am a woman-owned business, and I think that it's a great idea to bring more women on board.*

Everyone has a story, everyone has a bump in the road, everyone has a bad day, everyone has drama, everyone has family issues, everyone has dysfunction, everyone has something—but the world doesn't need to know about it. That does not mean that your story is not important, but your experiences and circumstances are personal, and although you want to use your personal explanation to justify a decision or circumstance, the two are mutually exclusive.

No one needs to know why you have decided to say no, especially if you have personal obligations that will not affect productivity and workflow. Yet, we volunteer unnecessary information. It's the subtle difference that turns a "no" into an explanation or substantiation of a decision. It also negates decisiveness and clear workplace boundaries. We are expected to provide more details, and the more that we volunteer an explanation and justification for every action, the harder it will be to ascend to the C-suite.

Learning how to keep it short and simple will help you self-assess your own defensiveness or reactive tones. When you communicate with a level of clarity and confidence, your team feels confident about your decision-making process under your leadership. But if you continue to negate the importance of trusting your intuition and leaning on your experience and expertise, the simplest answers become complicated. As discussed in Chapter 2, an important factor that contributes to the way women communicate beyond guilt is people-pleasing. We are worried about other people's feelings, and we are aware that no matter which way we lead, someone will impact our decision. As leaders, this fact is unavoidable. Not everyone is going to get what they want. Especially in negotiating, there are winners and there are losers, so it helps to be decisive.

How I Learned the Hard Way

In 2003, I was working at a medical malpractice firm. Some of the circumstances that people experience are extremely traumatic, from life-altering accidents in the operating room to infant death. Hearing the horrors of grieving mothers all day was my breaking point, so I decided I'd need to find a new job, quit, and never look back.

I interviewed for other positions daily during my lunch hour. I received a call from an outside subsidiary of American Express. Although I had not received the full offer from the company, I made the ultimate decision to quit my current job at the law firm because I was assured that I would get the job.

On July Fourth weekend in 2003, after only six months at the last firm, I made an impulse decision to walk over to my office manager and quit, while my supervisor was on vacation. I had already expressed some concerns to my office manager a few weeks prior, and since I did not hear a response from any of the partners, I knew that my back was against the wall. When I quit, I sat with my office manager and said, "I'm leaving. I want to thank you for the opportunity. I have already expressed my concerns in previous conversations, and silence is always a powerful answer." The entire time of this three-minute conversation, I was nervous, and there were moments where I almost cried because I wanted to explain everything that I was going through. However, I decided the best thing I could do was to keep it short and sweet. The only thing my office manager asked me was, "Are you coming in on Monday to give us all of the cases you are working on?"

I replied, "Yes, I will be here Monday and stay for a few hours."

On Monday, I took my items off of my desk and placed them in my pocketbook, then drafted a case list for the office manager. The song *Simple* by India Arie was playing in my head. I felt liberated and free. A few moments after my arrival, my office manager handed me two dozen roses and said, "We want to make a full announcement and allow everyone to say their goodbyes to you today." I instinctively knew that this opportunity for goodbyes would become one filled with my explaining my decision to people who didn't really want it or wanted to use my oversharing of my personal decision to talk me out of it.

"Thank you so much, but I must decline the invitation to express any gratitude at this time."

I knew that if I had explained my decision, nothing would have changed, and I would commit to a cycle of mental trauma by convincing myself that I could succeed in this role if I kept going. Worse, it would've shown that I was open to being convinced to change my mind, and I couldn't let that happen. Subsequently, it became clear that my decision to terminate my short-lived career was one of the best decisions I ever made. No one ever contacted me, sent me an email of good faith, or reached out to me to ask me anything. The quick and clean break was confirmation that to be direct without any emotional attachment is the way to emotional freedom and career redirection. Ever since I walked out of that office and into my navy-blue Honda Accord, I've never felt the need to explain myself to anyone ever again—no explanation required.

The need to explain or justify using emotional and highly personal processes doesn't only occur when you want to have some fun for yourself. Whether it be expanding your role within your organization, moving departments, going back to school, negotiating a major deal (or small one for that matter), or asking for the promotion, we need to tame how much we share, because when we focus too much on explaining the factors that galvanized us to the decision, we detract from the decision itself—and the value we bring to it. Giving the world an inside view into what you think and how you process your value, rather than being decisive and clear, is a surefire way to hand your power over to other people. You can see how overexplaining infiltrates the way women negotiate their raises, promotions, or business collaborations and transactions, which is detrimental to our career advancement. How can we win when we are being sorry for trying to win?

I used to feel the need to share more details about my life and decisions than necessary. I used to rehearse my story and practice with several of my enablers, which I called "friends." We would practice the "what if they ask you" scenarios, as I always felt the need to have layers in my story without leaving out any details. Then, I entered the "real world" with powerful leaders, and I learned that I was the only one talking. Once I realized no one was listening—and that nobody was ever going to ask whatever it was I was preparing for—I knew it was time to find a better way.

Consider the two versions of an email that follow:

Negotiating with the simple response:
Thank you for the response. We have received your counteroffer and will reply shortly.

The complicated and overexplained negotiation response:
Thank you for the response, and I apologize for taking so long to get back to you. I was out of the office yesterday on a field trip with my son and had limited access to my email.

I received your counteroffer, and I will review it today with the partners during our meeting this afternoon. I hope to have an answer for you by tomorrow, or at the latest, Friday.

Once again, accept my apologies for the late reply.

Thank you, (Your Name)

What Is Wrong with the Overexplained Version of This Email?

Let's start with the opening line, where the apologetic tone begins. Although innocent in meaning, opening a professional email to a stakeholder or client with an apology, followed by a personal circumstance, conveys a friendship context rather than business or professional dialogue. Unless the other party asked you if you were out of the office with your son yesterday, volunteering details beyond the scope of professional etiquette is not needed. The email uses limiting language, which minimizes your efficacy and professionalism. Also, it takes more energy to open an email with a narrative than one with a directive or deliverable.

A simple response, as sampled above, confirms receipt of the correspondence and the expectation of a counterresponse. It is pleasant, short, and effective. There is no need to explain your whereabouts or your personal life. All the other party needs to know is a method of following up further.

Achieving this level of confidence, clarity, and directness in negotiation and in any communication—professional or otherwise—does not happen overnight. One of the best tools and guideposts available to retrain yourself to keep it short and simple is what is known as the 8-Minute Rule. I use it to this day as a general practice.

The 8-Minute Rule

I learned about the 8-Minute Rule after spending a few years trying my hand at the world of venture capital. I always wanted to know why there weren't more women startup investors, especially in Silicon Valley. As a habitual researcher, I went out to find my answers, and it came down to what happens in closed-door pitch meetings.

During the height of the popularity of *Shark Tank*, there were a massive amount of *Shark Tank*–like incubators popping up around the world. Then, the Small Business Association began to host funding incubators for universities to teach students how to pitch their ideas to investors through incubator training programs. These incubators—including Y-Combinator, The Tory Burch Foundation, and Backstage Capital—allowed some of the world's greatest young minds to exchange ideas and learn how to become market-ready and competitive while understanding sales and valuation.

The first incubator I was privileged to attend was called Dibels, which was designed to specifically reach out to women and minority business owners, seeking partners to raise capital to fund purchase orders—orders on goods and services that must be fulfilled by outside vendors. The room was set up to replicate the hit reality show, and the audience had a chance to observe what a real pitch to a seasoned investor entails. The program was approximately six months long, and the participants spent another two months pitching day after day to the hungry investors. I went for the first three to four meetings and observed how investors watch the clock.

Participants each received eight minutes to explain to the potential investor their background, demonstrate their product, ask for an investment, and justify the valuation/ ROI. The investors made a hard stop at eight minutes. Time and time again, I watched women walk up to the center of the room and explain a long and drawn-out bio that exceeded the two minutes allotted for an introduction. Then, they spent time talking fast and speeding through their product without adding any value. As the clock approached seven minutes and 50 seconds, you would hear the nervous laugh of women saying, "Oh my gosh, time is running out, please, please, please." The investors would abruptly end the presentation on the eight-minute mark with "Thank you for your time," and call the next person. My heart would ache, because the presenters spent six months preparing for just eight minutes.

Proving your value in eight minutes is challenging. If the investors decided to give you an initial verbal offer, they would consider giving you more time to introduce yourself and talk about your background. However, the women participants spent most of the time on the introduction, and less time on the product. Some of the investors were women, and they did not engage in personal dialogue.

Reframe the time you have with decision makers as being the same as eight minutes pitching a product. Doing so helps you become more specific when articulating your goals during a conversation. If you want to accelerate to the C-suite, you will realize that the higher you go, the fewer conversations—especially containing small talk— you will have. Busy people simply do not have time to talk about the weather. You have to be structured, purposeful, and pointed with your conversations to ensure that you capture their attention early. Essentially, you have to get to the point.

When I interviewed Sheryl Sandberg for *Inc.* magazine, I had 10 minutes to complete the interview. She gave me the primary talking points. I asked three questions and produced a 1,200-word piece. I interviewed Ryan Serhant of the hit show *Million Dollar Listing New York*, and I had nine minutes of his time. In both scenarios, I did not have time to introduce myself or make niceties. The value of their time required us to focus on the deliverables only.

Do you think people like Oprah, Sara Blakely, Hillary Clinton, Melinda Gates, Stacey Abrams, or Bethenny Frankel have more than five to eight minutes to listen to your story? And I know you might be thinking, *they are far out of my reach.* Ironically, they are not out of your reach at all, that is a matter of perception, which we have discussed. Don't just think of them as a standard of admiration; their success is completely within your grasp if you know how to live by the 8-Minute Rule.

Let's go back to my example about the accident I had on my way to work. Would you have used your time explaining the accident, or would you have just stated the obvious: "I was in an accident and will not be in the office today"? I spent more time explaining the details of the incident than I did to explain my health and well-being. When I reevaluated that scenario, it was clear that I was looking for sympathy. I should've used one minute to explain the event, and only shared more if I was asked. The moment my office manager asked me the question, "Are you coming in today, yes or no?" She was thinking about the length of the conversation.

Every two minutes within the 8-Minute Rule requires a transition in the conversation or correspondence. Here's a breakdown to keep your communication short, sweet, and to the point (and we'll get to specific steps to make this happen shortly):

- The first two minutes of your conversation should focus on your intention and takeaways: what will the other person learn, and why is it important?
- The next two minutes are strictly presenting evidence to substantiate your deliverables.
- The penultimate two minutes are about you and why you are the most qualified.
- The last two minutes should be dedicated to your ask, request, or outcome.

If you want to extend the conversation or explanation, that needs to be on your personal time. In the context of the work environment, focus on strengthening productivity and less on developing a friendship. When decision makers know that you know the key components of an effective eight-minute conversation or correspondence, without the pomp and circumstance, they know that you value your own time.

Far too much I've noted how women are drawn toward a more emotional and personal story, while men do not rely on such tactics to shift opinions of others. Consider how you react to those who are long-winded and meander their way to a point, if any. The next time you are given a long-winded story, time the conversation and mark the transition points. Out of all of the details provided during the conversation, how many minutes did the person spend on the facts, which are germane to the decision-making process? Today, I normally reserve less than 10 minutes for outside conversations, and the first minute tells me everything I need to know.

Until I went into the venture capital world, I did not understand how to stop being a chatterbox. The conversations at the water cooler are not going to lead to the C-suite. When allies and sponsors are bringing names to decision makers about promotions or advancements, they pay attention to how much time is being spent on emotionally based conversations versus productive outcomes. Focusing on an 8-Minute communication and correspondence is crucial to understanding how effective leaders think, and how they process details.

Keep reminding yourself about the 8-Minute Rule. There are going to be moments when you don't even get an entire eight minutes, but if you are effective at grabbing people's attention within the first minute, even the shortest conversations will bring the most meaning to decision makers. You will find yourself explaining yourself less and becoming more productive. Every minute counts.

How to Create 8-Minute Micro Conversations and Connections

Here are the four steps to take to create an eight-minute micro conversation:

Step 1: Start with the End in Mind (2 Minutes)
It is normal to start conversations with polite gestures and greetings. However, value-based and value-add conversations must begin in reverse. Whenever you engage or correspond with decision makers, think about the intention or purpose of the conversation. What is the one value-add that you would like to leave with them? That should be your opening line in all correspondence and conversations.

For example:

- *"There is a new service that will increase productivity by 50 percent, and I need a moment of your time to discuss it with you."*
- *"I've found a way to increase our sales revenue and meet our numbers before the end of the quarter, and I think you would be interested."*
- *"There is a more efficient way to conduct our monthly meetings, which will save time and boost team morale, and I only need less than 10 minutes of your time to show you how."*
- *"I have some new ideas on improving our social media footprint using Instagram and TikTok, without the need for an outside ad agency, that will reduce our marketing budget while generating consistent sales."*

In every example, the objective is to avoid the personal introduction and focus on the deliverable. In each of the opening scenarios above, the objective is to capture the decision maker's attention by focusing on how you can provide a high-value skill that improves productivity. You will have time for introductions shortly, but the goal of your eight-minute conversation is to produce value at the beginning of the conversation to broker an introductory conversation.

Step 2: Present Proof (2 Minutes)

Take a page out of the hit movie *Training Day* when Denzel Washington's character Alonzo says, "It's not about what you know, it's about what you can prove." Substantiate your opening statement with facts or evidence of your value-add proposal. Although you may believe it is time for small talk, now is not the time to get off-topic. This is your moment to back up your opening statement. Always remember, once you have their attention, prove yourself fast. Don't lose momentum because you want to be friends.

For example, as continued from above:

- *"There is a new service that will increase productivity by 50 percent, and I need a moment of your time to discuss it with you." I recently attended a sampling session with XYZ software and have been using it for the past week. I have experienced amazing results, which has also helped alleviate the backlog we've had in data entry. It is user friendly and it will save us time on manual data entry.*

- *"I've found a way to increase our sales revenue and meet our numbers before the end of the quarter, and I think you would be interested." I found a new CRM that automatically tracks our new customer outreach and open rates for correspondence. It also tracks all of the conversion data and creates a spreadsheet for our department, which will avoid the need to train others on how to use spreadsheets.*

- *"There is a more efficient way to conduct our monthly meetings, which will save time and boost team morale, and I only need less than 10 minutes of your time to show you how." I have designed a template, where all of our managers can add sample questions, which will create an agenda for each meeting. Best of all, we can send out the agenda in advance to ensure every department is prepared with data and avoid follow-up notes after the meeting.*

- *"I have some new ideas on improving our social media footprint using Instagram and TikTok, without the need*

*for an outside ad agency, that will reduce our marketing
budget while generating consistent sales." There is a
new stock image site called XYF Imaging, where we can
download graphics, images, and MP4s, while purchasing
the royalty rights. Then we can add the voiceover and
upload without an outside agency.*

Step 3: Introduce Yourself (2 Minutes)

Once you present value up front, you win decision makers'
trust, so you can keep your introduction short. You will have
more time for a lengthy introduction as you build a solid
foundation with the gatekeeper or decision maker, but take a
moment to *brag* about your top attributes.

- *What makes your ideas valuable?*
- *How many years of reserved experience do you have?*
- *A sentence about your background*

Keep in mind, you are a walking, talking curriculum
vitae. Put your highlight reel on display. Mention all of the
impressive accomplishments and your career goals. The
reaction I want you to aim for in this two-minute conversation is "ahhhhh." This is your moment to brag without
shame or judgment because you have already proven that
you know how to create value up front.

- *"There is a new service that will increase productivity by
  fifty percent, and I need a moment of your time to discuss
  it with you." I recently attended a sampling session with
  XYZ software and have been using it for the past week.
  I have experienced amazing results, which has also
  helped alleviate the backlog we've had in data entry. It
  is user friendly, and it will save us time on manual data*

entry. I have been a sales director for over 10 years, with certifications from ABC University and additional training with MSD Sales Academy. During my tenure in this department, revenue has increased by 37 percent in the past year and is projected to exceed 60 percent by the close of next year.

- *"I've found a way to increase our sales revenue and meet our numbers before the end of the quarter, and I think you would be interested." I found a new CRM that automatically tracks our new customer outreach and open rates for correspondence. It also tracks all of the conversion data and creates a spreadsheet for our department, which will avoid the need to train others on how to use spreadsheets. I have a degree and training in information technology and coding, where I have developed software for RTM Corporation in San Francisco, California. I am always looking for software to improve workflow and avoid basic human errors, which can cause delays in growing the department.*

- *"There is a more efficient way to conduct our monthly meetings, which will save time and boost team morale, and I only need less than 10 minutes of your time to show you how." I have designed a template, where all of our managers can add sample questions, which will create an agenda for each meeting. Best of all, we can send out the agenda in advance to ensure every department is prepared with data and avoid follow-up notes after the meeting. I used to work in human resources before transitioning over to the training team, and the one complaint most teams have is the ineffectiveness of weekly meetings. For a few members on my training development team, it slows down productivity and impacts their morale to attend meetings without an agenda, so I wanted to try something to improve the experience for everyone.*

- *"I have some new ideas on improving our social media footprint using Instagram and TikTok, without the need for an outside ad agency, that will reduce our marketing budget while generating consistent sales." There is a new stock image site called XYF Imaging, where we can download graphics, images, and MP4s, while purchasing the royalty rights. Then we can add the voice-over and upload without an outside agency. I work with a few influencers to help grow their social media following, and I want to bring the same level of engagement to our company, without seeking an external firm, who may not report accurate numbers to our department. You can check out some of my work with other influencers on my Upwork platform.*

Step 4: Ask (2 Minutes)

This is the most difficult part of the 8-Minute Rule. I will confess that I used to struggle with this part of communicating in high-level circles. I was afraid to come across as a "user" or "greedy." I have learned, however, that successful people don't view you as competition. As long as you can present value, they are interested in collaborating with you. They will broker introductions and meetings for you without hesitation and help you grow your career.

You only have two minutes to ask for what you want or deserve, not what feels comfortable. If you would like a raise, promotion, or leadership role, this is the time to ask for it. So far, you have started the conversation with the goal, substantiated its value, and marketed yourself. This is the grand finale—what do you want? Stop thinking about humility; this is your moment to shine.

- *"There is a new service that will increase productivity by fifty percent, and I need a moment of your time to discuss it with you." I recently attended a sampling session with XYZ software and have been using it for the past week. I have experienced amazing results, which has also helped alleviate the backlog we've had in data entry. It is user friendly and it will save us time on manual data entry. I have been a sales director for over ten years, with certifications from ABC University and additional training with MSD Sales Academy. During my tenure in this department, revenue has increased by 37 percent in the past year and is projected to exceed 60 percent by the close of next year. With the right consideration (money/pay) or new designated title of VP of training and development, I will gladly take the lead in sourcing the software from the vendor and train my department to use the program within two weeks. It will add great results to our department and maximize our efficiency.*
- *"I've found a way to increase our sales revenue and meet our numbers before the end of the quarter, and I think you would be interested." I found a new CRM that automatically tracks our new customer outreach and open rates for correspondence. It also tracks all of the conversion data and creates a spreadsheet for our department, which will avoid the need to train others on how to use spreadsheets. I have a degree and training in information technology and coding, where I have developed software for RTM Corporation in San Francisco, CA. I am always looking for software to improve workflow*

and avoid basic human errors, which can cause delays in growing the department. I would like to discuss a pay per performance opportunity based on a three percent commission structure for all of our new clients who opt in using this new service.

- *"There is a more efficient way to conduct our monthly meetings, which will save time and boost team morale, and I only need less than ten minutes of your time to show you how." I have designed a template, where all of our managers can add sample questions, which will create an agenda for each meeting. Best of all, we can send out the agenda in advance to ensure every department is prepared with data, and avoid follow-up notes after the meeting. I used to work in human resources, before transitioning over to the training team, and the one complaint most teams have is the ineffectiveness of weekly meetings. For a few members on my training development team, it slows down productivity and impacts their morale to attend meetings without an agenda, so I wanted to try something to improve the experience for everyone. With the potential of shorter meetings, I am requesting flex-time to work from my home office at least one day per week to offset the time saved with our new agenda-led meetings.*

- *"I have some new ideas on improving our social media footprint using Instagram and TikTok, without the need for an outside ad agency, which will reduce our marketing budget, while generating consistent sales." There is a new stock image site called XYF Imaging, where we can download graphics, images, and MP4s, while purchasing the royalty rights. Then we can add the voice-over and upload without an outside agency. I work with a few influencers to help grow their social media following, and I want to bring the same level of engagement to our company, without seeking an external firm, which may not report accurate numbers to our department. You can check out some of my work with other influencers on my Upwork platform. I believe my proven experience for developing high-quality content, while building social campaigns that have reached over 5 million subscribers, on average, would be a great way to create a new role as social media and marketing manager, of which, I will onboard a team of proven marketing strategists to grow your brand globally.*

Ask and ask big. Never ask in layers—such as a trial offer or to work for free until you build trust. If you want a promotion, ask for it.

You can be just as effective, and polite, with a simple response. I know that it is difficult to detach the people-pleasing element from the way we engage, but I assure you that you can be just as effective with less. It is also important to remember that although mentorship is important, there are going to be situations when no one else is in the room except you. Self-discipline and accountability are going to be crucial. It's going to help you to memorize your triggers and learn when to have faith in yourself that yes or no is enough.

IT'S A WRAP!

You've just finished reading this book, and you're probably thinking to yourself, "When is the right time to start changing the way I communicate professionally?" The answer is today! The No Explanation Required lifestyle is achievable, but I want to make sure I leave you with my last tip—never wait for an invitation to communicate and express yourself. I have shared many experiences with you, but the most common experience I have witnessed is brilliant women who sit and wait for an invitation to speak and advocate for themselves—but the invitation never arrives.

Too often, women:

- Wait until the time is right
- Wait for someone to invite them to negotiate
- Wait for the right time to ask for time off
- Wait for the right time to advocate for ourselves
- Wait for someone to call on them in a meeting
- Wait for someone to invest in their brilliant ideas
- Wait to be asked to come and sit at the table
- Wait for an invitation that will never come
- Wait for someone to give them an invitation to speak up
- Wait to get another advanced degree or certificate to request a promotion
- Wait until they match all the qualifications in a job description

Now, you have the tools, and the skills, but no one will know how brilliant you are if you are always silent. Besides, silence is the wrong approach to accelerate your leadership journey. Leaders need to be seen and heard, but more importantly, you need to take initiative if you intend to get a chair in the C-suite. Any seat worth sitting in will require you to speak up and claim it. It will not be empty and awaiting your arrival.

Finding my voice and liberating myself from all of the childhood messages and discipline helped me become someone who feels powerful when I advocate for myself and others. I feel most powerful because I am no longer waiting for anyone to give me permission to speak, or to stand up on my behalf. I have found the strength to speak with a level of intention and authority without compromising my humor, thoughtfulness, or compassion. I have nonnegotiable boundaries, and remaining silent is not one of them.

I've gone from a prim and proper young girl, conditioned to be seen and not heard, to standing at the front of high-powered rooms in meetings and speaking up—the feeling is extremely rewarding, and still a bit intimidating. I was conditioned to seek validation and to be liked by others. On one hand, within my culture, I agree with a few of those principles in my personal life, but professionally, I realized I would never get to the C-suite without communication. As I'm writing this, women represent less than 10 percent of the C-suite. Although our fight is admirable, we need more women to collectively advocate and start normalizing the presence of women in the C-suite consistently.

Once I learned that communication was the only barrier between middle management and the C-suite, I directed more of my attention to holding myself accountable and communicating with authority. I have studied some of the best communicators, mostly men, and it was clear that they never explain themselves. Then, I remembered my middle school teacher and her lesson on prepositional phrases. It was as if someone screwed on the light bulb—no more explanations required after the preposition.

Keep in mind that No Explanation Required is a lifestyle, not just a phrase, because once you begin speaking up and communicating with clarity, it will change your life. Decision makers will look to you for guidance and leadership. You will attract leadership-level opportunities. Most importantly, you will begin to build your confidence. I'm learning that all of our conditioned behavior will take time to change, so be patient with yourself. It takes daily repetition and practice. Once you keep your ambitions in mind and consistently remind yourself to tap into your alter ego once in a while, you will find yourself simplifying your explanations and responses. You'll become less reactive and less apologetic. You will communicate with clarity, effectiveness, directness, and compassion—because it can all be done.

Where Do We Go from Here?

As you go forward, remember these key points:

- **Remember your prepositional phrases.** Keep your explanations brief and germane to the context of the conversation or questions.
- **Avoid pink perceptions.** We discussed how specific industries have been shaped by women; however, breaking the glass ceiling requires more than pink

perceptions and stereotypes. It is important to explore industries that are underrepresented by women. Shattering glass is about changing perceptions, not overcrowding the same professions. Think beyond the pink rooms.

- **Hold on to your pom-poms and start cheering for yourself.** It's time to promote yourself and show off your achievements daily. Use your last opportunity to attract your next opportunity, and stop depending heavily on a résumé to get into the C-suite. Network your way up the ladder, while bragging.
- **Tap into your Sasha Fierce.** It's time to channel your inner alter ego and create the confident persona that will help you activate your newfound level of confidence.
- **Respond, don't react.** It takes discipline to avoid reacting to a negative comment or criticism regarding work performance. However, a reaction could have long-term consequences. Take a moment to think about your response carefully.

To help you continue to grow your communication style, I am leaving you with communication starter scripts for a few common issues that arise in business and in the workplace. This will help you avoid the need to overcommunicate and overpersonalize, while remaining germane and focused.

SAMPLE SCRIPT

Salary Negotiation with a New Company

I would like to thank you for extending the (name the position) role, and while I am excited about the opportunity to work with a company that will productively utilize my skills and education, I believe the compensation package is not comparable to my competency level.

After careful research about the duties of the role as outlined, comparing salary data from (name your sources), and speaking with others with the same experience, education, and mastery, I have found that your initial offer is less than comparable for this position. Based on my research and findings, I believe (name your number) is a great place to commence my professional tenure with your company, and I welcome in-person evaluations every six months, which will also be followed by performance increase compensation.

Just to highlight, the unique skills that I bring to your company are:

- *Over 10 years of experience managing a sales team of over 100 agents, who were successful at meeting deadlines and quotas.*
- *I have increased the revenue of my former company by over 37 percent each year, by building a solid network of ready customers, who are committed to following me in this new role.*

- *I have brought in over 42 million dollars in new business opportunities for my company over the past 10 years.*
- *During my role as a team leader and manager, I had less than 10 percent turnover under my management.*
- *I have a degree from (name of school) and continue to engage in continuing education units to advance my leadership skills that will increase my value and productivity within the company.*
- *Since our initial conversation, I already have a few ideas I can share about how to increase revenue within the first six months.*
- *I am also looking for a company where I can grow and explore other challenging opportunities while putting my experience to the test, which is one reason I applied for this role.*

As such, I am aware of your budget/commitment for this position, but as I have highlighted, my background, education, and experience are closer to the market rate for the position, not an entry-level offer.

My counteroffer is _____

I look forward to your reply and the potential of adding value to the company

Avoid Generic Statements During a Negotiation Conversation

Don't use the following statements:

- *I am a trustworthy person*
- *I show up on time every day*

- *I am a fast learner*
- *I am a team player*
- *Money is not important to me*
- *I really need this job*
- *I know I can do the job*
- *I will take the low offer for now, but will you reconsider it later?*
- *Why is the offer so low?*
- *Is that your final offer?*
- *I would make a great employee*
- *Did you call my references?*
- *I can't work for that amount of money.*
- *I am a dependable person.*
- *Please?*
- *I thought the position paid more money?*
- *That's less than I thought.*
- *Is that the best you can do?*
- *Is it because I'm a woman?*
- *Is it because I'm "Black," "Latina," "LGBTQ," or my religion?*
- *How did you come to that decision?*
- *If you give me a chance, I'll prove that I'm worth more.*
- *Let me think about it.*
- *Let me talk it over with a few friends and get back to you.*
- *That was not the salary advertised.*
- *I will probably get a better offer someplace else.*
- *Is that all?*
- *I'm worth more than that.*

These are all phrases that I refer to as the generic plague of asking for what you deserve. They are often emotional and are more in line with begging and pleading, rather than stating substantiating facts to corroborate your compensation package. Remember, negotiating is about presenting facts, very similar to adjudicating a case in court. Presenting your unique value proposition in a very clear and concise format that highlights at least one financial gain for the new company will make the difference between taking the offer off of the table or getting the amended compensation that you deserve.

Avoid emotional statements in verbiage about who you are as a person. Remember the person on the other side does not know you personally, and a résumé or CV is a fictitious document that needs to be sold. Highlight all of your strengths, and always consider the replacement cost of losing your professionalism and contributions as a candidate.

In the mock scenario above, the main point that sticks out the most when encountering the offer is the $42 million in sales over 10 years. Numbers speak volumes to decision makers.

SAMPLE SCRIPT

Salary Negotiation for a Raise Within Your Current Position

I would like to discuss the findings of my most recent performance evaluation conducted last month. As noted during our conversation, we discussed how beneficial my work has been and the importance of my contributions within my current role. However, after much consideration, research, and thought, I believe that my contribution and tenure with this company needs to be reevaluated to consider a fair compensation agreement based on my current skills.

Since my arrival to the legal department, I have:

- *Reduced overhead and increased productivity by 38 percent over the past five years*
- *Assisted in evaluating, hiring, and training new staff to operate my department more efficiently, while adhering to strategic policies*
- *Developed the outreach arm of our department to follow up with clients regularly*
- *Suggested new software and CRM to manage client files*
- *Worked in a support capacity to assist the partners with the merger with X-Corporation*
- *Improved the overall performance of the legal department by focusing on intake management and increased revenue*
- *Implemented a strong profit-sharing system for client referrals, which has increased business by over 40 percent*

I have managed to become a trusted advisor and manager for my team and staff during my tenure with the firm. Although we have discussed a cost of living increase to my compensation agreement, I believe that my role has created significant positive changes for the firm, which can be easily measured.

Based on my research, other professionals in the area with my level of experience, education, and corporate growth are earning an average of 35 percent

> *more at this time. At this moment, we are still working*
> *off of the initial onboarding terms, which should be*
> *reconsidered with the above-mentioned factors in mind.*
> *I am requesting a 30 percent increase and*
> *consideration of remote work Fridays. This request is*
> *open for consideration for the next 15 days for your*
> *review, counteroffer, and/or feedback.*
> *I look forward to your thoughts.*

Similar to the previous list of "don'ts," keep your request strictly to the facts. Avoid generic statements such as:

- *I have been here for so many years.*
- *I'm a loyal employee.*
- *I just love what I do.*
- *I have been here longer than _____, and s/he makes more money than I do.*

Presenting facts is the best way to ensure the value of your proposal is met.

I want to highlight the importance of creating a timeline for responding as mentioned at the closing of the script. Open-ended requests for money are never a good idea, especially for women. Decision makers will have an elapsed time frame to find a way to create budget concerns or to use a personal circumstance against you to support their decision to decline your request. Hold them accountable for responding promptly, regardless of whether the decision is in your favor.

Quick tip—I advise that you also factor in the replacement value of your current role. In other words, when you are speaking with your HR department regarding a salary increase, it is worth mentioning the potential loss of revenue and productivity due to the loss of qualified talent.

SAMPLE SCRIPT
Requesting Fair Consideration
of Company Policies

Yesterday, I was approached by _____, who gave me an informal verbal warning about the company policy on checking my phone throughout the day.

I have been a committed member of this team for four years, and am well aware of the policy. I advised _____ that I needed to tend to a personal emergency, which will remain private. However, to avoid further misinterpretation of any professional misconduct or pressure, the company should forward an internal memo to all team members and reference the notation of the policy in the company manual to ensure equal access to the rule and consequences.

Thank you for your consideration,

SAMPLE SCRIPT

Request for Personal Time

Good Day,

I would like to submit my request to use my personal days on January 21st through January 24th.

As stated in the operations manual and revised company policy, personal days requested 45 days in advance are automatically accepted and all support staff are notified by Human Resources.

Thank you for your time,

Avoid adding unnecessary personal details, such as:

- *I have to travel to Arizona for my sister's wedding.*
- *I have three doctor's appointments.*
- *I am having new cabinet installed in my kitchen.*
- *My daughter has a dance recital in Texas.*

As long as you reference the company policy and remain within the guidelines of requesting your time, that is all that's needed.

SAMPLE SCRIPT
Request for a Management Role

I learned of a team lead opportunity in the operations department, which will be open in March, and I would like to be considered before HR posts an open call for candidates within the company.

I have worked with John Smith, who is the current operations supervisor, and I have attached his letter of support for consideration. My mentor, Jan Robins, who is also the chief financial officer, recommended me for the position, and she will become my director within the role. I will be an asset to the operations department, as I have five years of support experience and three years of training from XX University, with a concentration in management.

I would like to schedule a brief introductory call or meeting to discuss my qualifications.

Thank you in advance for your time.

SAMPLE SCRIPT

Request for a Mentorship

Good Day _____

I have learned so much from you over the years, and I continue to admire your work as I have watched you grow from accounting to chief marketing officer at XYZ Corporation.

I have reached a point in my career where I believe effective mentorship will help me develop my skills and prepare to transition into a leadership role within the next five years.

I am requesting a mentoring relationship where we can meet once per month. I am flexible with time considering your schedule. I would propose an agenda and forward the same two weeks in advance, so I can create an action list and report my progress.

I look forward to working with you and learning from your vast experience.

Thank you.

SAMPLE SCRIPT

Request for Workplace Boundaries

I would like to opt out of the on-call requests on Saturdays. I will not be able to participate due to personal obligations. If there is an emergency, please refer to the policy manual for contact information.
Thank you for honoring my personal request.

Avoid explaining the nature of your personal request and reason for opting out of a voluntary assignment.

Common Phrases to Avoid in Scripts

In all work-related discussions, avoid phrases like the following:

- *Because of my children*
- *Due to my religious beliefs*
- *Because it takes an hour to get home*
- *I've never asked for any favors, but . . .*
- *I love my job*
- *I need this job*
- *I need the money*
- *I need to make more money*

REFERENCES

Andrews, Shawn. "The Power of Perception: Leadership, Emotional Intelligence, and Gender." *Main,* August 18, 2016, https://www .td.org/insights/the-power-of-perception-leadership-emotional -intelligence-and-gender.

AP Archive. *U.S. Secretary of State Hillary Rodham Clinton's Temper Flared on Monday When a Congolese university student asked for her husband's thinking on an international matter.* YouTube, July 23, 2015, https:// www.youtube.com/watch?v=Y_2e9aC1ZUY.

Bartow, Ann. "Some Dumb Girl Syndrome: Challenging and Subverting Destructive Stereotypes of Female Attorneys." *William & Mary Journal of Race, Gender, and Social Justice,* Volume 11 (2004–2005), February 2005.

Bowles, Hannah Riley, et al. "Social Incentives for Gender Differences in the Propensity to Initiate Negotiations: Sometimes It Does Hurt to Ask." *Organizational Behavior and Human Decision Processes* 103 (2007): 84–103.

Brunner, Schatzie. "In Pursuit of Perfectionism." Schatzie Brunner (blog), December 1, 2016, https://schatziebrunner.com/the -danger-of-perfectionism/.

Bryner, Jeanna. "Key to Successful Marriage: Say 'Thank You'." Live Science, July 27, 2007, https://www.livescience.com/4556-key -successful-marriage.html.

Cardone, Grant. "Inspirational Sales Video Must Watch by Grant Cardone." YouTube, August 22, 2013, https://www.youtube.com /watch?v=DnKJDlaPI2c.

Carney DR, Cuddy AJ, Yap AJ. "Power Posing: Brief Nonverbal Displays Affect Neuroendocrine Levels and Risk Tolerance." *Psychol Sci.*, October 2010; 21(10):1363–8. doi: 10.1177/0956797610383437. Epub 2010 Sep 20. PMID: 20855902.

Chira, Susan. "The Universal Phenomenon of Men Interrupting Women." *New York Times*, June 14, 2017, https://www.nytimes .com/2017/06/14/business/women-sexism-work-huffington -kamala-harris.html.

"Cognitive Behavioral Model of Social Phobia (Clark, Wells, 1995)" (information handout), Psychology Tools, https://www .psychologytools.com/resource/cognitive-behavioral-model-of -social-phobia-clark-wells-1995/, accessed June 18, 2021.

Cooper, Marianne, "For Women Leaders, Likability and Success Hardly Go Hand-in-Hand." *Harvard Business Review*, April 30, 2013, https://hbr.org/2013/04/for-women-leaders-likability-a.

Cuddy, Amy. "Your Body Language May Shape Who You Are." TED, October 1, 2012, YouTube, https://www.youtube.com /watch?v=Ks-_Mh1QhMc.

Estrada, Jessica. "How Your Perception Is Your Reality, According to Psychologists" Well + Good, February 7, 2020, https://www .wellandgood.com/perception-is-reality/.

Fairchild, Caroline. "For Women, Being 'Liked' at Work Is a Double-Edged Sword." LinkedIn, July 31, 2019, https://www .linkedin.com/pulse/women-being-liked-work-double-edged -sword-caroline-fairchild/.

Farber, Madeline. "What Happens to the Wage Gap When Women Hit 32." *Fortune*, June 22, 2016, https://fortune.com/2016/06/22 /gender-gap-widens-age-32-study/.

Forchheimer, Shannon. "Beware the Female Biglaw Partner." But I Do Have a Law Degree (blog), October 31, 2011, http://www .butidohavealawdegree.com/2011/10/beware-female-biglaw -partner.html#.YC6ahWhKhPa.

Gallo, Amy, "How to Give an Employee Feedback About Their Appearance." *Harvard Business Review*, May 26, 2017, https://hbr.org/2017/05/how-to-give-an-employee-feedback-about-their-appearance.

"Girls Trip (2017)" IMDb, July 21, 2017, https://www.imdb.com/title/tt3564472/.

Gupta, Alisha Haridasani. "The Likability Trap Is Still a Thing." *New York Times*, November 22, 2019, https://www.nytimes.com/2019/11/22/us/the-likability-trap-women-politics.html.

Harbinger, AJ. "7 Things Everyone Should Know About the Power of Eye Contact." Business Insider, May 14, 2015, https://www.businessinsider.com/the-power-of-eye-contact-2015-5.

Hauser, Robin. "The Likability Dilemma for Women Leaders." TEDxMarin, TEDx Talks, November 8, 2019, YouTube, https://www.youtube.com/watch?v=PYyBqs_x044.

Hinshaw, Stephen, and Rachel Kranz. *The Triple Bind: Saving Our Teenage Girls from Today's Pressures and Conflicting Expectations*. Penguin Random House, 2009, see https://www.penguinrandomhouse.com/books/80356/the-triple-bind-by-stephen-hinshaw-phd-with-rachel-kranz/.

Hockenbury, D., and Hockenbury, S.E. *Discovering Psychology*. New York: Worth Publishers, 2007.

Jamula, Jen, and Goldberg, Allison. "Step up to 2020 with an Alter Ego." Forbes, September 16, 2020, https://www.forbes.com/sites/jenjamula-allisongoldberg/2020/09/16/step-up-to-2020-with-an-alter-ego/?sh=50a5d4193200.

JCI Foundation. *Carla Harris - Perception Is the Co-Pilot to Reality*. YouTube, 18 Aug. 2016, https://www.youtube.com/watch?v=RF6Z0aBo3P0.

Jovanovic, Maja. "How Apologies Kill Our Confidence." TEDxTrinityBellwoodsWomen, TEDx Talks, February 13, 2019, YouTube, https://www.youtube.com/watch?v=G8sYv_6uyss.

Kross, Ethan, and Bruehlman-Senecal, Emma, et al. "Self-Talk as a Regulatory Mechanism: How You Do It Matters." *Journal of Personality and Social Psychology*, 2014, Vol. 106, No. 2, 304–324, http://selfcontrol.psych.lsa.umich.edu/wp-content /uploads/2014/01/KrossJ_Pers_Soc_Psychol2014Self-talk_as _a_regulatory_mechanism_How_you_do_it_matters.pdf.

Kruse, Michael. "The TV Interview That Haunts Hillary Clinton." POLITICO Magazine, September 23, 2016, https://www.politico .com/magazine/story/2016/09/hillary-clinton-2016-60-minutes -1992-214275/.

Madell, Robin. "The Self-Promotion Gap Is Holding Women Back at Work—Here's What to Do." *U.S. News*, November 27, 2019, https://money.usnews.com/money/blogs/outside-voices-careers /articles/the-self-promotion-gap-is-holding-women-back-at -work-heres-what-to-do.

Meckler, Laura, and Peter Nicholas. "Hillary Clinton's Forgotten Career: Corporate Lawyer." *Wall Street Journal*, October 28, 2016, https://www.wsj.com/articles/hillary-clintons-forgotten -career-corporate-lawyer-1477674562.

Newton-Small, Jay. "Is Hillary Clinton 'Likable Enough?'" *Time*, May 25, 2016, https://time.com/4347962/hillary-clinton-donald -trump-likability/.

Nicholas, Peter, and Byron Tau. "Hillary Clinton Officially Becomes First Woman to Win Major Party Nomination." *Wall Street Journal*, July 26, 2016, https://www.wsj.com/articles/hillary -clinton-officially-becomes-first-female-to-win-major-party -nomination-1469572814?mod=article_inline.

O'Leary, Kevin. "Shark Tank Star Kevin O'Leary's Morning Routine - A Day in the Life of a Multi-Millionaire." YouTube, May 7, 2020, https://www.youtube.com/watch?v=iWKb5WHQJMg.

Partners Advantage. "How Your Professional Appearance Affects Productivity and Confidence." Partners Advantage (blog), January 25, 2017, https://blog.partnersadvantage.com/how-your -professional-appearance-affects-productivity-and-confidence.

Robson, David. "The 'Batman Effect': How Having an Alter Ego Empowers You." BBC Worklife, August 17, 2020, https://www .bbc.com/worklife/article/20200817-the-batman-effect-how -having-an-alter-ego-empowers-you.

Ryan, Lisa. "For Women, the Quest for Perfection Can Lead to Depression." The Cut, October 10, 2016, https://www.thecut .com/2016/10/for-women-the-quest-for-perfection-can-lead-to -depression.html.

Sandberg, Sheryl, and Adam Grant. "Speaking While Female." Women at Work, *New York Times*, January 12, 2015, https:// www.nytimes.com/2015/01/11/opinion/sunday/speaking-while -female.html.

Sankar, Carol. "I'd Rather Be Respected, Than 'Liked.'" Medium, March 10, 2017, https://carolsankar.medium.com/the -confidence-factor-for-women-i-would-rather-be-respected -9171658ae820.

Sankar, Carol. "The Motherhood Recession." *Entrepreneur*, September 9, 2020, https://www.entrepreneur.com/article /355045.

Saujani, Reshma. "Teach Girls Bravery, Not Perfection." TED: Ideas Worth Spreading,TED2016, February 2016, https://www .ted.com/talks/reshma_saujani_teach_girls_bravery_not _perfection?language=en.

"The Self-Promotion Gap." The Self-Promotion Gap, https://www .selfpromotiongap.com/home. Accessed February 18, 2021.

60 Minutes. "Hillary Clinton's First 60 Minutes Interview." YouTube, August 28, 2019, https://www.youtube.com/watch?v= -UqKNgrwK8E.

Tavakoli-Far, Nastaran. "Naomi Osaka Apologizing for Winning Is the Other Tragedy of the U.S. Open." *The Lily*, September 12, 2018, https://www.thelily.com/naomi-osaka-apologizing-for -winning-is-the-other-tragedy-of-the-us-open/.

Torres, Monica. "This Chrome Email Plugin Wants You to Stop Saying 'Sorry' All the Time." Ladders, June 28, 2018, https:// www.theladders.com/career-advice/this-chrome-email-plugin -wants-you-to-stop-saying-sorry-all-the-time.

"US Open Winner Naomi Osaka Speaks Out on Controversial Serena Williams Match." TODAY.Com, September 10, 2018, https://www.today.com/video/us-open-winner-naomi -osaka-speaks-out-on-controversial-serena-williams-match -1316645443687.

Women in the World. "Viola Davis' Full Interview with Tina Brown at the Women in the World Los Angeles Salon." February 15, 2018, YouTube, https://www.youtube.com/watch?v= PXI5eXBZoZs.

"Wondering About Zoom Etiquette?." The Women's Journal, June 16, 2020, https://womens-journal.com/wondering-about-zoom -etiquette/.

INDEX

Abrams, Stacey, 180
Accomplishments:
  dismissing your own, 32–33
  gender differences in
    promoting, 143
  listing your own, 19–21
  sharing your own, 34
Addressed, how you should be,
  66–67
Adele, 81
Alienation, 31
Alliances, with other women,
  110
Alter egos, 75–90, 194
  benefits of, 84
  and fear of public speaking,
    75–77
  and gender expectations, 2–3
  and respect in workplace, 59
  steps to create, 84–90
  tapping into your, 81–84
  and thinking of yourself in
    third person, 78–80
Amazon, 25, 30, 31, 33, 98
Anxiety, 148
Apologies, 137–157
  and Emotional Freedom
    Techniques, 147–153

and gender, 141–147
  making unnecessary, 137–141
  replacing, with gratitude,
    154–157
Appearance:
  and alter ego, 87
  importance of, 45, 53–54
Apple, 98
Ask, presenting your, 181,
  187–190
Asset, making yourself, 71–72
The Atlantic, 145
Attraction, psychology of, 56
Authenticity, 74

Backpedaling, 109
Backstage Capital, 178
The Balancing Act, 20
Bartow, Ann, 94
"The Batman Effect" (Robson),
  77
BBC, 77
Because, 160–166
Behavioral response, to
  emotion, 116
Behaviors:
  avoiding self-limiting, 46–50
  unlearning of, 84–85

Belonging, in the room, 79
Best Buy, 33
Beware the Female Biglaw Partner (blog), 145
Beyoncé, 81, 107
Blakely, Sara, 19, 180
Boll, Jamie, 20
Boundaries:
  and "nice" girls, 104
  request for workplace, 205
  that build respect, 66–71
Bragging:
  and feminine modesty, 144
  learning to, 32–34
  in micro-conversations, 185–186
  power of, 8–9
  and self-promotion, 22–28
Brown, Amanda, 95
Brudz, Steve, 143
Bruner, Pamela, 148
Bryant, Kobe, 81
Business Insider, 48

Cherry, Kendra, 115
Chess, 131
Chira, Susan, 107
Clark, David M., 76–77
Clinton, Hillary, 180
Coca-Cola, 134
Columbia Business School, 20
Communication, 113–135
  in alter ego, 88–89
  being less reactive in, 123–125
  bragging as, 22, 33
  closed, by leaders, 30
  with confidence, 89

cost-benefit analysis, 133–135
  effected by Covid-19 pandemic, 13–14
  emotional element of, 115–117
  and leadership, 7–8
  and networking, 9
  nonverbal (*see* Nonverbal communication)
  reactive, 117–123
  responsive, 125–129
  and silence, 130–133
  steps to respond effectively, 129–130
  of your worth, 13–15
"Communication in the Real World" (University of Minnesota), 42
Company policies, requesting fair consideration of, 201
Complex prepositions, 162–163
Confidence:
  and alter egos, 79, 87
  and apologies, 150
  and bragging, 26
  communicating with, 89
The Confidence Factor for Women, 6–7, 13, 37, 89, 164
Confidentiality, maintaining, 69
Consistency, in sharing your accomplishments, 34
Control, of yourself, 122
Conversations:
  micro- (*see* Micro-conversations)
  simplicity in, 190

taking initiative to engage in, 49–50
Cooper, Marianne, 64
Corcoran, Barbara, 19
Cost-benefit analysis, in communication, 133–135
Covid-19 pandemic, 13–14
Criticism:
responding with gratitude towards, 156
and success, 119
C-suite:
and apologetic behaviors, 142
communication skills for, 192–193
effective communication necessary for, 169
influencing perceptions of gatekeepers for, 42–43
and others' perceptions of you, 54
women in, 3–4
Cues, for habits, 152–153
Culture, gender expectations and, 1–3
Currency, bragging as, 25
Cutraro, Erin Loos, 61

Decision-makers:
communication style viewed by, 122–123
earning respect of, 71
gratitude when talking to, 155
making connections with, 85
making yourself an asset to, 72

quality of conversations and, 182
silence as signal for, 132
staying in your lane to attract attention of, 74
Decisions:
effective communication of, 171–172
explaining with prepositions, 160–161
Deliverables, focus on, 183
Details, unnecessary, 176–177, 202
The Devil Wears Prada (film), 64
Dey, Rohini, 98
Dibels, 178
Distancing, with alter ego, 83–84
Double Dutch jump rope, 55–56
Duhigg, Charles, 150–153

Education Connection commercials, 99
8-Minute Rule, 178–182
Emails:
composing responses to, 124
gratitude in, 155
prioritizing, 68
Emotional Freedom Techniques (EFT), 147–153
Emotional statements, in negotiations, 196–198
Emotions:
and communication, 115–117
and habits, 153
putting aside, 90

"Emotions and Types of Emotional Responses" (Cherry), 115
Encyclopedia of Strategic Leadership and Management, 143
Energy frequency, changing, 149
Entrepreneur, 21, 25
Estrada, Jessica, 40
Evidence, presenting, 181, 183–185, 200
Expectations, setting, 72–73
Explanations:
  and gender, 5
  learning to stop providing, 15
  offering unnecessary, 171
  overexplaining, 177
  and prepositions, 160–161
Eye contact, 48

Facebook, 20, 27, 86, 98, 125–126
Fair considerations of company policies, 201
Fairchild, Caroline, 60
Family, women's care of, 93
Farber, Madeline, 93
Fear:
  communicating with, 28
  and negotiation, 164
Feminine modesty, 143–145
50 Cent, 134
"Fight or flight" reactions, 116
First impressions:
  importance of, 37–40
  making great, 53–54

First person, speaking in, 24, 33, 48–49
Fitting in, 74
Focus, on yourself, 24
The Food Network, 98
"For Women, Being "Liked" at Work is a Double-Edged Sword" (Fairchild), 60
"For Women Leaders, Likability and Success Hardly Go Hand-in-Hand" (Cooper), 64
Forbes, 8, 20, 21, 25, 51, 78
Forchheimer, Shannon, 145
Forgive to Win! (Jacobson), 32
Fortune, 93
Frankel, Bethenny, 180
Frankel, Lois, 100

Gallo, Amy, 38
Gatekeepers:
  engaging in conversation with, 50
  influencing perceptions of yourself by, 42–43, 46
  making yourself an asset to, 72
Gates, Melinda, 180
Gender:
  as adjective of profession, 97–98
  and apologies, 141–147
  and self-promotion, 28–32
Gender expectations:
  and being "nice," 91–92
  and culture, 1–3
  and success, 64

at work, 11–12
in workplace, 60
Gender wage gap, 93
Generic statements, avoiding,
    196–198, 200
Girls:
    expectations for, 1–3
    and pink perception in
        upbringing of, 105–106
    teaching feminine modesty
        to, 144–145
Girls Trip (film), 104
Glamour, 21
Glass cliff, 74
Goals, setting, 85–86
Grant, Adam, 108
Gratitude, replacing apologies
    with, 154–157
Grey Horse Communications,
    29
Guilt, 173

Habit, apologizing as, 149
Hall, Regina, 104
Harbinger, AJ, 48
Harris, Carla, 43
Harvard Business Review, 38,
    64
Harvard Business School, 20,
    150
Harvey, Steve, 20
Hauser, Robin, 63
Hedging, apologies as, 141
Hinshaw, Stephen, 106
Housing and Urban
    Development
    Redevelopment Fund, 47

"How Apologies Kill Our
    Confidence," 150
"How to Give and Employee
    Feedback About Their
    Appearance" (Gallo), 38
"How we form habits, change
    existing ones." (Wood), 151
"How Your Perception Is
    Your Reality, According
    to Psychologists"
    (Estrada), 40
How Your Professional
    Appearance Affects Your
    Productivity (Time
    Management Ninjas), 54
Hustle Harder, Hustle Smarter
    (50 Cent), 134

Ice Breaker conversation
    starters, 50
IGI Global, 143
Inc., 19, 21, 25, 27, 49, 125, 180
"Increase Your Ask," 163–166
Incubators, 178–179
India Arie, 174
Insecurities:
    communicating, with
        apologies, 142
    dealing with, 75–77
    and nonverbal
        communication, 102–104
Intentions, setting, 71–73, 181
Interruptions:
    continuing after, 109
    by men and women, 107–108
Introductions, 181, 185–187
It Takes Two, 56

Jackson, Curtis, 134
Jackson, Selma, 10–11
Jacobson, Walter E., 32
James, Lebron, 81
JCI Foundation, 43
Jet.com, 30, 31
Johnson, Dwayne, 81
Jordan, Michael, 81
Jovanovic, Maja, 150
Just Not Sorry app, 143

Kakwani, Manish, 143
KISS principle, 169

TheLadders.com, 143
Language:
    avoiding self-limiting, 46–50
    and backpedaling, 109
    as intentional tool, 134–135
    minimizing, with apologies,
        143
Leaders:
    downplaying roles of, 23–24
    as problem solvers, 79–80
    reactive vs. responsive, 14
    as responsive communicators,
        117
    women as, 3–4, 100
Leadership:
    and communication, 7–8
    and likability, 63
    look for roles in, 69–70
    and performance under
        pressure, 83–84
Lean In, 125
Legally Blonde (film), 95
Liability, becoming, 72

Likability:
    and apologies, 145
    pitfalls of, 61–63
    psychology of, 63–65
    respect vs., 60–63
    "The Likability Dilemma," 63
    "The Likability Trap Is Still a
        Thing" (Cutraro), 61
The Lily, 144
Limitations, 5
LinkedIn, 60
Listening, in interviews, 10
Lists, making, 68
Live Science, 142
Long-term thinking, 124
Lopez, Eric, 9
Lunch meetings:
    building relationships with,
        68–69
    setting expectations for,
        72–73

Management role, request for,
    203
Manufactured identities, 81
MC Lyte, 55
McKinsey & Company, 125
Meetings:
    gratitude when talking in, 155
    lunch (*see* Lunch meetings)
Mentorship, request for, 204
Meridian points, 148, 149
Micro-conversations, 167–190
    8-Minute Rule for, 178–182
    steps for creating, 182–190
    unnecessary information in,
        169–177

Microsoft, 98
Mighty Forces, 29
Million Dollar Listing New York, 19, 180
Mindset, 40
Modesty, 143–145
Momentum, in conversations, 184
Morgan Stanley, 43
MTV Awards, 107

"Naomi Osaka apologizing for winning is the other tragedy of the U.S. Open" (Tavakoli-Far), 144
"Nasty" woman, becoming, 107–111
Negotiation:
    prepositions in, 163–166
    sample scripts for salary, 195–196, 198–200
    women's reluctance to engage in, 93–94
Networking, 9–11
New York Times, 55, 107, 108
"Nice," women as, 91–93, 100–106
Nice Girls Don't Get the Corner Office (Lois Frankel), 100
Nicknames, 66–67
No Explanation Required lifestyle, 193
Nonverbal communication:
    eye contact, 48
    and insecurities, 102–104
    and perceptions, 40, 51–54
    pose, 52–53

posture, 51–52
smiling as, 100–102
Nursing, 99

O, The Oprah Magazine, 25
O'Leary, Kevin, 19, 49
On Your Side Tonight with Jamie Boll, 20
One Sheet, 27–28
On-topic, remaining, 128, 129
Opportunities:
    increasing, by bragging, 24–25, 28, 34
    and perceptions, 40
    prepositions in conversations about, 163–166
    responsive approach to, 134–135
Oprah, 21
Oprah Effect, 18
Organizational Behavior and Human Decision Processes, 93
Osaka, Naomi, 144
Overcoming Fake Talk (Stoker), 51
Overpracticing, 110–111

Passive communication, 14
    avoiding, 130
    in negotiating, 164
    reactive communication as, 120
Passive prepositions, 160–162
Pauses, in communication, 123–124
People-pleasing, 173

Perceptions, 37–54
  definitions of, 42
  importance of, 37–40
  influencing others', 45–50
  and nonverbal
    communication, 51–54
  of others, 40–43
  self-perception, 44–45
Performance, 42–43
Personal time, requests for,
  202
Personality profile, of alter ego,
  87–89
Phrases to avoid, 205
Physiological response, to
  emotion, 116
Pink (singer), 81
Pink perception, 94–100, 194
Poses, 52–53
Posture, 51–52
The Power of Habit (Duhigg),
  150, 152–153
Power poses, 52–53
Prepositions, 159–166, 193
  complex, 162–163
  in opportunity conversations,
    163–166
  passive, 160–162
Pressure, performance under,
  82–84
Prioritization, 67–70
Problem solvers, leaders as,
  79–80
Productivity, 67–70
Professionalism, 127
Professions:
  gender as adjective of, 97–98

marketed toward women,
  95–96, 99
Proof, presenting, 183–185
Psychology of likability, 63–65
PsychologyTools.com, 76
Public speaking, 75–77, 110, 156

Reactions, 117–123, 194
  learning to avoid, 123–125
  negative consequences of, 115
  responses vs., 114–115
Real estate investments, 61–63
Reality, perception and, 43
Reclaiming your time, 70–71
Reiss, Tami, 143
Relationships:
  building, with lunch
    meetings, 68–69
  in building companies, 89
  with work colleagues, 57–58
Remunerative value statement,
  35–36
Replacement value, 35, 200–201
Representation, of self, 41
Respect, 55–74
  boundaries that build, 66–71
  creating, in routines, 71–74
  likability vs., 60–63
  mixed messages about
    earning, 57, 65
  and psychology of likability,
    63–65
Responses, 125–129, 194
  and Covid-19 pandemic,
    13–14
  deciding when not to respond
    at all, 132–133

reactions vs., 114–115, 120
steps for effective, 129–130
Responsibility, for other's
perceptions, 40–41
Résumés, 12–13, 26–28
Reviews, sharing your own,
33–34
Rewards, for apologizing, 152
Risk-aversion, 104–105
Road rage, 120
Rob Base, 56
Robson, David, 77
Role models, for girls, 1–2
Routines:
changing habits in, 151–152
creating respect in, 71–74

Salary negotiations, 195–196,
198–200
Sample scripts:
for fair consideration of
company policies, 201
request for management role,
203
request for mentorship, 204
request for personal time, 202
request for workplace
boundaries, 205
for salary negotiations,
195–196, 198–200
Sandberg, Sheryl, 20, 108, 125,
180
Saying no:
lack of explaining when,
165–166
and respect, 73
Schumann, Karina, 141–142

ScienceDaily, 151
Self-limiting language and
behaviors, 46–50, 140
Self-perception, 44–45
Self-promotion, 17–36
and bragging, 22–28
and communication, 13–15
gender gap in, 28–32
instead of résumés, 12–13
learning to brag, 32–34
and perceptions, 43
remunerative value
statement, 35–36
The Self-Promotion Gap, 29
Serhant, Ryan, 19, 180
"7 Things Everyone Should
Know About the Power of
Eye Contact" (Harbinger),
48
Shark Tank, 19, 49, 178
She Should Run, 61
Sia, 81
Silence:
and communication,
130–133
and learning to speak up,
191–192
as response, 130
Simple, 174
Small Business Association, 178
Small talk, 179
Smiling, 100–102
Smith, Jada Pinkett, 20
"Social incentives for gender
differences in the
propensity to initiate
negotiations," 93–94

Social media, 86, 118–119
Social phobia, 76–77
Society for Human Resource Management, 99
Socioeconomic norms, gender and, 99–100
"Some Dumb Girl Syndrome" (Bartow), 94–95
Southpaw Insights, 29
Speaking up, by women, 107–111
"Speaking While Female" (Sandberg and Grant), 108
Standing up, 52, 109
The State of Black Women in Corporate America, 125
Staying in your lane, 73–74
"Step Up to 2020 with an Alter Ego," 78
The Steve Harvey Show, 20, 21–22, 24
Stoker, John, 51
Strategy, importance of, 131
Subconscious mind, role of, 32
Subjective experience, of emotion, 115–116
Success:
  and criticism, 119
  perceptions of women with, 64
  and respect, 59–60
Survival-level businesses, 98
Survival-level careers, 99
Swift, Taylor, 107

Tapping, 147–153
Tavakoli-Far, Nastaran, 144

TED Talks, 19, 52, 63, 150
TEDx events, 21; 27
Temper tantrums, 122
Templates:
  for replacing apologies with gratitude, 154–156
  for trigger interactions, 123
Terms of endearment, 66–67
Tesla, 98
"That will never happen for me" mindset, 80
Third person, thinking of yourself in, 78–80
"This Chrome email plugin wants you to stop saying 'sorry' all the time" (Torres), 143
Tillberg, Eric, 143
Time:
  reclaiming your, 70–71
  taking adequate, in effective responses, 129
Time Management Ninjas, 54
Timelines, for responses, 200
Toastmasters, 110
The Today Show, 20, 24, 144
Torres, Monica, 143
The Tory Burch Foundation, 178
Training Day (film), 183
Triggers, recognizing, 123
The Triple Blind (Hinshaw), 106
Trust:
  and perceptions of others, 41, 54
  and respect, 65

Unique value proposition (UVP), 128, 198
"The Universal Phenomenon of Men Interrupting Women" (Chira), 107
University of Minnesota, 42
University of Southern California, 151
Unlearning, of behaviors, 84–85
Upstream Analysis, 29
U.S. News, 28
UVP (unique value proposition), 128, 198

Value:
in conversations, 182–183
proving in 8 minutes, 178–179
Vanzant, Iyanla, 148
Vermilion Restaurants, 98
VeryWellMind.com, 115
Vitamin Water, 134

Wage gap, 93
Wall Street Journal, 21, 55
Well+Good, 40
Wells, Adrian, 76–77
The Wendy Williams Show, 19
West, Kayne, 107
Why Do Women Bully Each Other at Work?, 145
"Why Don't More Women Negotiate?" (Sankar), 20
"Why Women Apologize More Than Men" (Schumann and Ross), 141–142

William and Mary School of Law, 94
Williams, Serena, 144
Williams, Wendy, 19
Winfrey, Oprah, 18, 180
Women:
alienation of other, due to self-pride, 31
in the C-suite, 3–4
lack of support from other, 145–146
marginalized, by pink perception, 95–96
supporting other, 110
Women@ Leadership Day, 20
Women-centered stereotypes, 91–111
becoming a "nasty" woman, 107–111
perpetuation of, 100–106
and pink perception, 94–100
Women's Summit, 49
Wood, Wendy, 151
Workplace:
emotions impacting you at, 116
expectations for behavior in, 65
reactive communication in, 121–122
relationships in, 57–58
request for boundaries in, 205

Y-Combinator, 178

Zuckerberg, Mark, 45

ABOUT THE AUTHOR

Carol Sankar is a guest contributor and writer, a powerful public speaker, and the founder of The Confidence Factor for Women. Best known for her talks on confidence and negotiation for women, her research has been quoted online by Harvard University and the Society for Human Resource Management. She has also been quoted in several leading publications, including *Politico, Business Insider, Glamour*, and *O, The Oprah Magazine. Forbes* also named her as one of the leading voices on diversity and inclusion.

Carol has been featured by hundreds of media outlets including Forbes, *Inc.* magazine, *Entrepreneur*, the *Wall Street Journal*, A&E, NBC, CBS, ABC, and CNN Money. She has also given talks at TEDx, SXSW, Facebook, Harvard Business School, Columbia Business School, The United Way, and more. Carol is a proud wife and mother, active real estate investor, and advisor.